THE LEADERSHIP LIBRARY
VOLUME 9
WHEN TO TAKE A RISK

THE LEADERSHIP LIBRARY

Volume
9

When to Take a Risk

A Guide to Pastoral Decision Making

Terry Muck

Carol Stream, Illinois

WORD BOOKS
PUBLISHER
WACO, TEXAS

A DIVISION OF
WORD, INCORPORATED

WHEN TO TAKE A RISK

Library of Congress Cataloging in Publication Data

Muck, Terry, 1947-
When to Take a Risk

(The Leadership Library ; v. 9)
Bibliography: p.
1. Clergy--Office--Decision making.   2. Risk-taking
(Psychology)   I. Title.   II. Series.
BV660.2.M83   1987   253′.2   86-26912
ISBN 0-917463-12-9

Printed in the United States of America

In faith she married.
Yes, Judy loved me.
But love pledged a lifetime
risks all.

CONTENTS

INTRODUCTION
WHITE-WATER
PEOPLE

In one of his sermons, Bruce Thielemann, pastor of First Presbyterian Church in Pittsburgh, Pennsylvania, quoted a champion surfer who had spent years mastering his sport: "There is a need in all of us for controlled danger, for an activity that puts us on the edge of life."

"Living on the edge of life" is one way to define risk. Risk taking occurs when we put our reputation, beliefs, financial security, personal well-being, or even our lives on the line. We may do so simply for the thrill. Or we may do so in the hopes of achieving some higher goal — as Samuel Johnson said, "to risk the certainty of little for the chance of much."

Thielemann used the surfer analogy to challenge Christians to risk safety and security for the chance of doing much for the kingdom — confronting a fallen world with the gospel's radical message. Only by a willingness to "paddle out to where the white water is" can we hope to meet the mandates Christ gave us for serving a world in chaos.

The challenge of white-water thinking, applied specifically to pastors and local church leaders, was the motivation for this book. I knew from my experience as editor of LEADERSHIP, a quarterly journal for 100,000 pastors on the front lines of

Christian ministry, daily, indeed hourly, local church leaders face the realities of confronting Christians as well as a non-Christian culture with true Christianity. Difficult decisions, involving daily risk to their well-being and the well-being of their churches, are commonplace for pastors.

Yet I also knew from conversations with hundreds of pastors in churches of different denominations across the country that few view themselves as risk takers or white-water people. They know they have difficult jobs and they are thrilled to serve so fully in Christian ministry. They have a deep desire to be effective, but they are generally reluctant to analyze closely their daily decision making. And the idea that daily they are taking risks, although not entirely foreign to their thinking, is not the common way they express it.

With this background, I set out to answer two sets of questions.

Why are pastors uncomfortable with the concept of risk taking?

How *do* pastors view the difficult decisions they make? As risks? As simply the tough realities of the task God has given them? What happens when disaster strikes?

To answer these questions, Virginia Vagt, director of corporate research at Christianity Today, Inc., and I developed a survey asking pastors about the toughest decisions they have made in ministry and how those decisions worked out. Did their decision solve the problem? Or did it lead to worse problems, pain, disillusionment, and perhaps even dismissal? What were the personal and professional costs of such decisions? In retrospect, would they do anything differently? We mailed the survey to a random sample of 1,000 LEADERSHIP subscribers. The results were computer tabulated and analyzed. (More details of our research technique are in the Appendix.)

The results of our research form the basis for much of this book. My impression that pastors rarely think about their difficult decisions as risks was confirmed. Yet they recognized after the fact that risk was involved all along. When risk was described simply in terms of difficult decision making (as we did on the survey), the respondents immediately recognized themselves and their situations in the questions. Further, nearly unanimously they desired help in making more informed decisions.

Would using the concept of risk help?

The second set of questions revolved around the concept of risk. Would pastors be helped by recasting some of their decision making into the language of risk analysis? Would a better understanding of risk help or hinder the decision-making process?

To answer those questions, I began to read the secular literature on risk taking. I applied some of the concepts to the local church setting, and then went out and conducted personal interviews with pastors, asking them how useful these concepts of risk taking would be in their churches.

From the survey, I learned much about the different kinds of decisions a pastor is called upon to make and the relative risk of each. Virginia and I put together a "risk profile," a short series of analytic questions to help pastors identify the degree of risk associated with various decisions they must make. (See Chapter 13.)

From the in-depth interviews, I gathered stories and examples of pastors taking risks in ministry, and how they analyzed those difficult decisions. This reaffirmed my impression that viewing difficult decisions in the language of risk would be helpful.

In many ways the results of the interviews and survey must be viewed as provisional. We gathered an enormous amount of anecdotal material that we have attempted to quantify. We have even tried to show some statistical tendencies in the form of charts and our risk profile. But they are tendencies only, offered to help pastors begin to ask the right questions about tough decisions they face regularly.

Nothing is as distinctive as the problem you are facing today, complete with its own set of church members, circumstances, and spiritual dynamics.

Often I let the stories and anecdotes speak for themselves, with little attempt at statistical quantification or even analysis. I offer these stories as models, both positive and negative, in hopes that you will identify the transferable principles to guide your own ministry.

My prayer is that as you read this book, you find yourself in it. Through the stories of church ministry, I want to affirm you as one of God's front line officers, facing the enemy at close range, reinforced by the knowledge that thousands of others all over the globe are leading soldiers against our common enemy. Reinforced, too, by the understanding that we are fighting in God's army, and through Christ we will be the eventual victors over sin and disappointment.

ONE

THE RISKY BUSINESS OF MINISTRY

Security is mostly a superstition. It does not exist in nature, nor do the children of men as a whole experience it. Avoiding danger is no safer in the long run than outright exposure. Life is either a daring adventure or nothing.

HELEN KELLER

We are not used to thinking of ministry in terms of risk. Risk implies an element of doubt and uncertainty. It suggests dangerous initiative. Risk is a frontier word, a word borrowed from the arenas of war and business.

Religious propagators, on the other hand, tend to present the church as a risk-free zone, a haven of rest floating on clouds of salvation. This view has understandable roots. God has promised us the security of eternal life. Where is the risk in such certainty? Many of us have sung the Daniel Whittle hymn: "I *know* whom I have believed / and am *persuaded* that he is able / to *keep* that which I've *committed* / unto him against that day" (italics mine). No uncertainty there. With such an absolute theology, it is only natural to think that a church, properly functioning, hums along without the risk associated with the secular world.

Intuitively, local church leaders know different. They know the gut-wrenching decisions they are forced to make and the pain a misstep, or even the proper step, can bring. They have made many difficult decisions and waited for the conse- quences — occasionally peaceful resolution but more often explosions of varying magnitude.

In spite of such crises, the popular image of the church as a smoothly operating temple of God's Spirit remains strong. It is an image all of us would like to believe, so we sometimes work on two different planes. On one level, we present a smoothly functioning façade to the world (occasionally even in our own thinking), all the while trying to cope behind the scenes with the reality of administering a complex church institution — a task that requires every bit as much skill as handling a small business.

Thus, too often the image of harmony, good and worthy in itself, hinders the strong, direct initiative called for in the everyday functioning of the body of Christ. Would coming to grips with the concept of risk taking help?

The following story of one pastor and his antagonist can be read two ways. It can be read passively, without the notion of risk, with only the feeling that *this kind of thing should never happen in the body of Christ*. That disavowal, as we shall see, is itself why many of these skirmishes escalate into full-scale war.

Or it can be read actively, with an eye to danger and decision, putting yourself in the place of Pastor Stoller, and asking: *What would I have done differently? When would I have taken a stand? When would I have risked the short-term pain of a difficult decision in anticipation of long-term health?*[1]

A Case History

Al Stoller always relied on two things to work himself out of tight spots — his gift for dealing with conflict and the belief that God would take care of people problems. So when trouble surfaced in the person of Pete Mankin, Al figured things would work out.

Al, with his wife, Marcy, had been pastoring the Christian Church in Hamilton, Ohio, for eight years when they met Pete. Hamilton is a town of seven thousand west of Pittsburgh, and Pete was a local businessman whose factory employed many of the people in the church. They met when a flood damaged a dozen houses in the neighborhood where many of Pete's employees lived.

Al's congregation had a disaster unit. When a house burned or a barn collapsed, the unit would offer food and assistance. Following this flood, they brought in tractors and trucks and brooms and buckets to clean up. Several days after the flood, Pete heard from his employees how the Christian Church people had helped. So he dropped by the church and asked, "Who are you? Why are you helping these people?"

The Mankin family started attending Al's church. It began to make a difference in Pete's life. He had been living in the fast lane, but soon opened his home for a Bible study. Then he became involved in the administration of the church's grade school and served on its board of directors, eventually becoming chairman.

"We recognized right away he was a strong man," remembered Marcy. "He had charisma, which made it easy for people to take his side, even if they didn't really believe in what he was doing. He was attractive and warm in many ways."

"He was generous," said Al. "He and his wife had a large house and would have the whole congregation in for a pizza party. He even bought a bus for our Christian school — a twenty-thousand-dollar gift."

The first year after Pete joined the church, everything went smoothly. He continued to grow spiritually. He initiated men's Bible studies at his home or at restaurants. He would stand up on Sunday and tell the people how much they meant to him. Al felt they had found a strong leader. He remembers telling Marcy one Sunday evening, "Pete is really growing. I can see him being an elder of the church one day."

Pete's spiritual growth, however, proved selective. Certain areas of his life remained untouched by repentance and grace, particularly the material side of life. He had lots of money and enjoyed spending it on comforts and entertainment. He did a lot of expensive traveling. He was known as a sharp businessman, occasionally too sharp.

"It's hard to describe the problem I began to sense. So much of it dealt with his motives," said Al. "Pete was outwardly supportive of the church, but he did things that made me wonder.

"For example, I would preach about fairness in our financial dealings with others, and Pete would nod his head. But then he would tell me privately how great it was that he could pay his employees so little. He said he wouldn't be able to compete in the Pittsburgh market, but here the rural environment enabled him to get cheap labor and make good money."

Al suggested that Christian managers should want employees to benefit when the company benefits.

"These people are happy with what they have," snapped Pete. "They wouldn't know how to handle more money if they had it. They're just grateful for a job, and that's what I'm giving them. If I weren't here, where would they be?"

Soon Al realized that Pete was telling his employees a different story. "Some of the employees who attended our church reported that Pete would go through the shop and say, 'We're having a bad year, guys. We've got to do better. We need more production.' At the same time he would be telling me how much income he'd made this year, and how great the bottom line looked."

Pete's sharp business practices extended beyond low wages, however. Although others in the church didn't know much about Pete's business ethics, he took Al into his confidence, probably out of a need to engage in the executive's version of locker-room talk.

"He told me things that I kept confidential. But I would tell him how I felt about those things. He didn't like that, of course. He would tell me, 'You've never been in business, so you can't possibly understand all the issues.'

"This put me in an awkward position. I felt a need to keep it in confidence, because I didn't want to prejudice the church against an immature Christian. But I also realized some of the things he was doing, particularly where they affected other members of our church, had broader implications than Pete's own spiritual well-being. The church would eventually be adversely affected."

The trouble started shortly after Pete announced he wanted to make his business a Christian establishment. Calling his workers together he said: "I want my business to be run the same way we run the church — by New Testament principles. I may have been lax in this in the past. But from now on I want to run not only a profitable business, but one that is as ethically sound as any organization there is."

That sounded great. But pretty soon the men from the church who worked for Pete started telling Al: "He still swears like a sailor. And he mocks leaders of the church, both the elders and the pastor."

Al asked them why they hadn't told him this before.

"Before, we put up with his double standard because we all do it to some extent," one young engineer confided, "but his grand announcement was too much. Announcing he's going to run his business by Christian principles — and then not changing anything — is pure hypocrisy."

That was Al's first sign that all was not well between pastor and nascent disciple. Viewed alone, that would have been disturbing, but not enough to keep Al awake at night. But other collisions of the pastor's sphere with Pete's sphere began to make Al wonder if he wasn't involved in a game that had more at stake than simple competitive pride.

For example, the principal of the church's grade school resigned. Attempting to aid the search for a replacement, Al, as the church's chief administrator and thus ex officio member of the board, suggested a teacher from the staff. An excellent teacher, who had been with the school from the beginning, she had just gotten her master's degree in school administration. She wanted the job and was fully qualified. Pete, however, started the rumor that Al was twisting his arm and trying to take over his job as board chairman.

Marcy, not knowing Al had recommended this teacher, also recommended her to Pete. Pete then told his friends that Al was using his wife and "several others" (the church secretary had also talked to him) to sway him.

"It was simply a case where there was one logical, qualified candidate, and everyone recognized that — except Pete," Al said later.

In the end, Pete didn't consider the teacher, and she left to teach in another private school. That was a loss; dedicated teachers were hard to find. Even after she left, Pete persisted in implying that Al tried to twist his arm.

Al finally talked to the elders of the church about Pete. "Of our four elders, two were cautious about Pete and were aware of some double-dealing; the other two were favorable toward him, and they soon let Pete know I was raising questions about him.

"Another time we were building a new building and some people were painting at night. We needed lights and used some stage lights Pete had loaned the school stage troupe. He got angry about the lights being used that way. I offered to buy new lights, and he said no. But he continued to tell people how he resented it.

"These all sound little, but I felt a growing conflict. I should have dealt with it, but I let it slide, hoping it would go away."

The conflict was beginning to take its toll on the pastor's home life. Marcy noticed all was not well.

"I was aware of what was going on, but not its intensity," she said. "Al would tell me some things people were telling him, and I couldn't understand how Pete could lead two such different lives. How could he keep from tripping himself up? How could he remember what he said to someone at work and not contradict himself at church?"

Gradually the emotional anguish became more obvious.

"I knew Al was struggling, and my intuition told me big trouble was brewing. I knew two of the elders would have a hard time standing up to Pete, so when Al mentioned setting up a retreat with the elders to determine what direction to go, I was all for it."

The elders went on retreat in the Poconos in March. Things appeared to go well. Al outlined the growing conflict with

Pete, and after discussion the head elder told him, "We don't see any problem with your ministry — let's just keep working at this." Even the two who were more supportive of Pete agreed that Al was the person to support.

When the elders came back and told the church they were in full support of their pastor, Pete started coming on strong. He began to tell members of the church, "If you aren't men enough to stand up to the pastor and get him out of here, I will."

Six weeks later one of the elders came to Al and said, "I'm withdrawing my support from you."

"What changed your mind?" Al asked.

The defecting elder didn't have an explanation.

Again Al remembers that as a time he should have acted: "I knew the elder was withdrawing his tithe from the church, and he acknowledged his loyalty was withdrawn. I should have asked him to step aside until the problem could be worked through. But I didn't."

The next Sunday, Pete stopped Al after the service and said, "If you don't leave the church, I will." Al could only stammer something about those not being the only alternatives, but he knew he was in for a battle.

The pressures mounted. At a church business meeting, Pete told the congregation, "The Lord has told me it's time we got new leadership. The time has come for Pastor Al to move on."

Apparently, God hadn't been telling any one else in the congregation; Pete's reasoning came across as unclear and arbitrary. The people didn't know how to take Pete's "message from God." No action resulted.

For Al, the message was especially confusing: "I'm not sure what was the root of his motivation to have me ousted. Theologically, we disagreed over prosperity teaching. Pete would say things like, 'The more money you give, the more you'll get back.' It affected the way we did some of the business of the church. I told him, 'Pete, I believe the Bible says the Lord is going to give back to us, but not necessarily in dollars. And that's a low motivation for giving.'

"He was particularly disturbed when I said in the pulpit that I disagreed with a preacher I had heard say, 'God gave his Son in order to get more sons.' To me, God's love is so pure that if only one person had responded he would still have loved. He didn't give his Son only to get a greater return on his investment.

"Yet I can't believe theology was the real reason. Much of it was personal, I'm convinced. He knew I was learning more and more about his business practices, and that made him uneasy. I learned that in order to get rid of his plant manager, he accused him of having an affair with someone in the office. There was no basis to the accusation. The man did leave the plant, however, with a broken life.

"Few people in the congregation were aware of what was going on, and I didn't tell them. The elders and I didn't know how public to make it. Now I see it was weak leadership on my part that I didn't do something publicly. We had disciplined people who were unfaithful sexually and released them if they were unrepentant. We should have followed the same procedure in this case. Pete's actions were just as harmful spiritually and should have been dealt with.

"Yet if we had confronted Pete with these things, he would have gone to any length to convince people they weren't true."

Once an employee at Pete's business overheard him talking on the telephone about the pastor: "We almost have him broken down. Just hang in there. We'll get him to resign yet."

Al asked Pete to come to an elder's meeting and there he asked him about the story. "That's a big lie," Pete said. "My entire office staff will deny it ever happened. I'll swear on the Bible it didn't happen."

There was a pause, and one of the elders said, "Pete, you may not like this, but you did make that telephone call and say those things. I was the one you called."

Pete started to backpedal. "Boy, I don't remember saying that." But he was caught red-handed.

Al let his defenses down. The battle was the Lord's, and the

Lord would win the battle. Hadn't the elder, one of his opponents, held Pete to account? Surely they all could see what kind of man they were facing. But Al hadn't seen the end.

In the middle of May, two days before Al and Marcy were set to leave for their vacation, another elder withdrew his support from Al.

"That didn't give us time to do anything," remembers Al. He told Marcy, "We can't leave now."

But the other two elders urged Al to go: "We will keep things under control until you get back." They wanted Al to get the rest he needed.

"We did need the time off. Because of the day school, I worked seven days a week. I was really tired. So we went."

Shortly after Al and Marcy left, there was a death in the congregation. Al flew home for the funeral and immediately sensed things were not well. He performed the funeral Sunday afternoon and was told the church was having a congregational meeting that evening — and he wasn't invited. Their reason: "Things that need to be said can be said in your absence."

Al flew back to Vero Beach, Florida, where they were staying with friends. When Marcy saw him, she immediately knew something was wrong. "We walked the beach, and Al was beside himself. Being in the dark about what was going on made everything seem a hundred times worse than it might have been. Finally he said, 'If the people can't see what's going on, maybe we ought to resign.'

"Al felt betrayed by the elders. He couldn't bear the tremendous gulf between himself and the congregation he'd been so close to. I was angry at God a little myself for what it was doing to Al. Many nights I would lie awake listening to him sob in his sleep."

Finally Al called the chairman of the elders and said, "I'm going to give it another twenty-four hours of thought, but I think I'm going to resign."

"Boy, that's going to be hard," said the elder, "but that's up to you."

After thinking about it for one day, Al called the elder and dictated a letter of resignation that he wanted read to the congregation. "The elder told me later he cried that night, but he didn't say anything then. He felt I was resigning for my health, and he didn't want to talk me out of it. I felt he wasn't supporting me, that Pete had gotten to him, too. I knew this man had a heart for the church, and if he didn't think I should stay, I didn't want to. If he didn't want me to resign, I didn't get the message."

By December, Al and Marcy left the congregation they loved and cared for. To this day they both feel their work there was left unfinished.

"Marcy had told me in March we should leave, and I had said, 'I won't run from trouble. We've had difficulties before, and we've always worked through them.' She felt this was different, but I still think we could have prevented it, and I also think I made too hasty a decision. I walked away from a lot of people who didn't know what was going on and who would have jumped to my support if they had seen the whole picture."

*　　*　　*

Al has done a great deal of reflecting on what happened: "What could I have done differently? A lot of little things, I suppose. But I can think of two major things that might have made a difference:

"First, I could have taken the risk of confronting the situation much sooner. I might have lost the battle with this powerful man earlier, but I doubt it. It would have been better to act early and perhaps get my nose bloodied than to wait until my entire ministry was at stake.

"Second, I could have involved more people and told more of what I knew. I felt a responsibility to keep in confidence things I knew were going on. Now I feel that when sin is occurring in a parishioner's life, the elders should know about it."

Two months after Al and Marcy Stoller left the church, Pete

Mankin left also. Several months later, the two dissenting elders left. A behind-the-scenes power struggle decimated the leadership and left a church full of bewildered people wondering what happened — and why.

What to Do?

What happened to Al and Marcy Stoller is replayed someplace almost every week. A powerful person or group in the church develops a dislike for the pastor, and over time the bad feelings escalate to warfare and dismissal, resignation, or church split. Even in milder cases of conflict, bad feelings and hours of wasted ministry time leave the church weakened.

What can be done? Al recognized he needed to take the risk of confrontation sooner. He didn't because it would have involved a fight. There was a chance, however small, that the conflict would have dissipated without confrontation. But there was a chance it wouldn't have. How could Al have gauged the relative probabilities of the two possibilities?

It was possible Pete would have a miraculous change of heart. It was possible he would leave the church of his own accord. It was possible someone in the church, a strong elder perhaps, could have seen what was going on and put an end to Pete Mankin's shenanigans. It was also possible no one would notice what was happening until it was too late. What resources do beleaguered pastors have, and how can they measure the strength of them?

Knowing when to act decisively in hard situations is one of the arts of ministry. It can make the difference between productive ministry and spending all one's time putting out fires.

Not that aggressive decision making will remove hard decisions. No amount of wisdom removes the risk from ministry. There will always be Pete Mankins ready to challenge the integrity of the work and our right to do it. Nothing will change that.

Risk is part of church life, just as it is part of everyday life. Everyone tolerates a certain amount.

But it is possible to avoid being paralyzed by the prospect of risk. *Understanding* risk helps strike the best balance between opportunity and fear. There is no opportunity without risk, but there can be risk with minimal fear.

Similarly, understanding the relative riskiness of various church decisions will make us more comfortable with those decisions, and thus more efficient and effective in making them.

TWO

LEARNING ABOUT RISK

The blind man is not afraid of ghosts.

BURMESE PROVERB

Al Stoller's decision not to take the risk of confrontation differs little from an executive neglecting to make a decision because he can not or will not recognize the long-range implications.

Several years ago an executive faced a difficult decision at his chemical company's coking plant. Coke making requires a gigantic battery to cook the coke (a derivative of coal) slowly and evenly for long periods. The battery is the most important and expensive piece of equipment used in the process.

This particular plant's battery showed signs of weakening. A replacement would cost $6 million. Such a large expenditure would adversely affect the bottom line that year. Pressured by a recent corporate decree to cut unnecessary expenditures, the businessman tabled the request to replace the battery. Instead, the existing battery was patched and held together for four more years.

When the battery finally collapsed, however, the company, unable to produce coke for several weeks, was sued for breach of contract by a steel producer. The Environmental Protection Agency cited the firm for violating pollution regulations. Eventually, the total bill, including lawsuits and replacement, exceeded $100 million.

In hindsight, of course, we can see the executive should have replaced the battery earlier. Had he acted decisively, millions of dollars would have been saved. He took what appeared to be the risk-free way — and ended up risking not only his leadership but the very existence of his business.[1]

Contrast that account of indecision with a story told about Calvin Coolidge. During his term as governor of Massachusetts, the Boston police force went on strike. The police commissioner responded by recruiting a new force. Samuel Gompers, president of the American Federation of Labor, appealed to Coolidge to recognize strikers' rights. Coolidge dictated a reply: "There is no right to strike against the public safety by anybody, anywhere, any time."

Friends urged Coolidge not to send it, saying it would end his political career. "Very likely," said cool Calvin, and he sent the message anyway. It proved to be a successful, and popular, decision.

Such commitment under pressure inspires. The contrast between our close-to-the-vest executive and daring Coolidge appears to teach a simple lesson: act decisively and with bravado.

But is it really so simple? When we stop to think, we recognize that in the case of a prudent, successful politician like Calvin Coolidge, for every risk he took there were ten he did *not* take because he judged the danger too great. In fact, Coolidge's biographer later noted that "Coolidge was the reluctant hero of law and order. Only with great caution did he recognize the issue that had been forced on him by the Boston Police Strike."[2] Coolidge did indeed stick to his guns — but out of careful deliberation, not any John Wayne bravado.

How does one judge the relative riskiness of a decision? When do you take a risk? Answering those questions demands that we look more closely at what risk is.

Risk Is Inescapable

We go to great lengths to avoid risks, especially physical ones. Entire government agencies protect us in the work place, on the highways, and aboard public transportation. Other agencies guard our food, drugs, and medical care. Educational institutions are monitored to protect us from psychological risk and manipulation.

With this apparent cushion of protection around every facet of our lives, we are tempted to think of ourselves as safe. Two factors, however, betray the illusion.

The first is our own secret yearning for the zest that risk brings. Something deep in our psyches tells us it is better "to put all, save honor, in jeopardy" than to look too long before taking a leap.

The second factor is reality itself. Risk is still an inevitable part of daily life. Death, the ultimate risk, lurks on the edge of everyone's consciousness. We take a risk every time we drive a car, eat a meal, meet a new acquaintance. Unknown contingencies challenge every waking moment.

The illusion of risk-free living weakens our ability to cope when danger, either physical or psychological, does strike. August Heckscher, in the *Christian Science Monitor*, said that perhaps the primary aim of education is to make informed risk takers: "Every graduate from the ideal school should be constantly undertaking ventures that test him and put his very being in hazard. What he learns from his books and teachers is not information, certainly not technical knowledge. It is a sense of the values that make him what he is and that may permit him to become somebody different. It is an instructed judgment and a capacity to dare. . . .

"To be a risk-taker requires a mature perception of our changing position amid complexities. If an acquaintance is to turn into a friend, and a friendship into a deeper intimacy, one must be aware at each stage of what is happening in one's inner and outer world. Shakespeare described the nobility of life as being able 'to look before and after,' to appreciate, that is, precisely the pitfalls one is escaping and the rewards one achieves."[3]

Once the ubiquitous nature of risk is understood, we become better decision makers. Instead of forfeiting opportunity by doing nothing at all, we can choose between actions, accurately weighing the risk of each.

Risk Is Essential

Without risk takers, life would be even more dangerous. Politicians, doctors, and scientists throughout history who were willing to take well-calculated risks have benefited us all. Smallpox was the scourge of mankind in 1717 when Zabdiel Boylston developed an effective but hazardous method of protection. He called it *innoculation*. He injected a small amount of infected material directly from smallpox patients into uninfected patients.

It was reasonably effective. During previous epidemics of smallpox, one in seven of those infected died. Only one in forty-one of those Boylston innoculated died. Boylston did not lack volunteers for this risky procedure because fear of the epidemic drove people to him. Boylston's medical colleagues, however, strongly opposed his revolutionary practice. They made a great deal of the one of his forty-one patients who died, ignoring the extraordinary improvement in mortality the other forty represented.

They accused Boylston of violating two of the ancient injunctions of Hippocrates, whose teachings had guided medical ethics since antiquity: "Above all do no harm to anyone nor give advice which may cause his death." Boylston persevered in his treatment because he understood the relative risks of not being innoculated (at epidemic's end, 844 of 5,759 people, or 14.6 percent of those who developed smallpox, died) compared to the risks of being innoculated (eventually 6 of 247 people, or 2.4 percent of those he innoculated, died).

This striking reduction in the risk of death eventually exonerated Boylston and demonstrated the principle that smallpox could be prevented by human intervention, eventually leading to the almost-foolproof method of vaccination.[4]

It also illustrates the principle of benefiting from a thorough understanding of risk.

Risk Is Necessary in the Church

Risk taking is a necessary part of local church ministry. Without risk-taking leadership, churches quickly become ineffective. The great leaders of church history recognized this and took great risks to further the cause of the body of Christ. Two examples:

John Chrysostom. A Christian orator, Scripture exegete, and church father, Chrysostom was born at Antioch about 347. After ordination as a priest in 386, he began a brilliant preaching career. In his zeal to keep the church pure, however, he frequently called the clergy to task. He berated the rich in his congregations for not regarding their wealth as a trust, and charity to the poor their chief obligation.

This was a risky position to take in a day when Christianity was the state religion, endorsed in all its pomp and luxury by the Empress Eudoxia. Eudoxia was known for both her support of the Christian clergy and her luxurious lifestyle. Surely Chrysostom understood the risk of attacking not only the church hierarchy but the empress. After weighing the risks, he decided it sufficiently important to take the chance. As a result he was exiled by Eudoxia and was deposed as bishop by the clergy.

Was it worth the risk? Eudoxia is now a footnote to history, the other clergy of the period mostly unknown. Chrysostom's writings, however, have influenced countless theologians in the fifteen centuries since his death.[5]

Ulrich Zwingli. In 1522, Ulrich Zwingli had been preaching the gospel in Zurich for three years. Shortly after Ash Wednesday that year, Zwingli made a symbolic stand regarding the rule of fasting from meat during Lent.

Zwingli attended a simple evening meal at which some of those present ate sausage. Although he did not eat any himself, he raised no objection, an equal sin for a clergyman. It would have been easy for him to escape the consequences. He could have explained it as a mistake or admitted it as sinful and sought absolution.

Instead, Zwingli not only condoned the action but made it a public issue in his sermon of March 23, which was enlarged on April 16 into a short pamphlet. In that pamphlet he explained that he had never spoken against abstaining from eating meat during Lent or on Friday. What he had encouraged, he said, was freedom in Christ, and this had been interpreted by some to imply they need not abstain from meat. It was this opinion regarding freedom in Christ, rather than the action taken, that Zwingli sought to justify.

Eventually the Swiss church adopted Zwingli's position, which led to a more unified church in Switzerland and contributed to the reformation of the church throughout Europe. Zwingli accomplished this by risking his name and position on the matter.[6]

We could go on with further illustrations of risks taken in local churches throughout the ages. Risk is part of life and ministry. Indeed it might be accurate to say that to minister well is to know when to take risks.

THREE

WHY WE'RE AFRAID TO TAKE RISKS

Fear nothing but sin.

GEORGE HERBERT

What is it about the human psyche that makes risk taking so difficult?

Much of the scientific research on the subject has been done in decidedly nonecclesiastical settings — gambling casinos. Psychologists Gideon Keren and Willem Wagenaar, for example, observed more than eleven thousand hands of blackjack played by 112 gamblers in an Amsterdam casino, attempting to analyze how the players made their judgments. They found most players were reluctant to take large risks, and attributed the generally conservative play to three factors:

— Minimizing regret. Busting (taking one card too many and going over the game's limit of twenty-one points) was avoided. Better to let the dealer win than to be the cause of your own loss.

— Delaying bad news. Because the dealer plays last, players would rather lose at the last possible instant rather than force their own loss by acting too soon.

— Attentional bias. Players tended to work harder to avoid losing than to figure the best way of winning.[1]

Each of these reasons holds obvious implications for leaders. Leaders, like gamblers, tend to delay the decisive action needed in a risk-taking situation.

Leaders in the local church often add one more factor to this list — the reluctance to face personal confrontation. When we asked our survey respondents to list the biggest hurdles they have in making difficult decisions, they often expressed this fear:

— "I have a strong aversion to confrontation."

— "It's the nagging, building anxiety I hate the most."

— "I'm afraid of the challenges to my authority such a decision seems to inevitably bring."

— "I just dread the people hassle."

Thus, in spite of its importance, most local church leaders find making risky decisions difficult, because it often means clashing with a church member. Even when pastors gather enough courage to make the confrontation, and even when it is successful, many have trouble taking any satisfaction in it because of the temporary conflict it creates. Tom Monitor, pastor of the Meadowland (Virginia) Baptist Church, remembers such a confrontation:[2]

"When I came here, two families controlled the church. One man had been first elder for twelve years, and a husband and wife team had been the Sunday school superintendent and treasurer, respectively, for eleven years. The control was so tight that when I went to the treasurer and said, 'I'd like to know our financial standing and policies,' she said, 'I've been around the church a lot longer than you have, and I'm going to give you a little advice: You take care of the preaching, and I'll take care of the finances.'

"That early conversation set the stage for our relationship. From then on I was 'that arrogant seminary student who thinks he can run the church.'

"I learned the Sunday school superintendent/treasurer couple played a little game every year. When the nominating committee would ask them to continue serving, they would say, 'No, we'd better resign' . . . but it was well understood they didn't mean it and just wanted to be begged to serve again. In the past, the pastor had dutifully done so and returned them to office.

"So my first spring in the church, when they said, 'We're not going to run for our positions this year,' I said, 'OK, we'll find somebody else.'

"Then I went to the congregation and said, 'Ralph and Martha have decided not to run again for their positions. Let's thank them for their many years of service, and let's begin as a congregation to pray about who God wants to serve in these positions.'

"What had been a cold war with this couple suddenly became hot. Several meetings with them, the first elder, and two other elders ensued, the stated agenda was to find out what the problem was between them and me — why I was not willing to work with them. But we all knew what was really happening.

"For one of those meetings, the superintendent's wife sent a list of grievances with her husband. The first one was that I did not give a monthly report of my activities at the board meetings as called for by the constitution. The first elder said, 'Well, I can tell you why he doesn't do that. I've never told him about it.'

"The next grievance was that I spent money that wasn't approved by the board, the third that I wasn't willing to work with the people who had always been in charge of the church. I explained that a minister must have the authority to spend certain monies without calling a board meeting and showed how the accusations lacked any substance.

"After reading the first three, and listening to my responses, the superintendent folded his paper and put it back in his pocket. Sometimes the ideas you come up with in the privacy of your own home fall flat when exposed to outside air. At least, that's what the superintendent seemed to feel, and the meeting ended shortly after that.

"But the couple soon took up the battle on another field. They sent a letter to all the denominational officials they could think of: general superintendent, district superintendent, former district superintendent, first elder of this church, third elder of this church. The letter said, 'We are charter members of this church, and we have always been able to work with other pastors. But we have been unable to work with Reverend Monitor. Therefore, we are resigning our memberships.'

"The responses I got back were almost all supportive. My general superintendent called to say, 'Tom, I just wanted you to know that I often get letters like this, and I threw this one in the trash can. Then I prayed that God would make you strong in a negative situation.' "

The strangling power structure of Tom Monitor's church was finally broken. The church has prospered since then, largely because he had the courage to confront the manipulative couple. Without confronting the situation early in his tenure, he may have faced a far worse situation down the road. With the risky confrontation, however, he went through short-term pain and discomfort. But he created a better ministry for the majority of church members.

Why don't more pastors face the need for such risk taking? There are many reasons.

Personal Insecurity and Other Hang-ups

Tom Monitor, despite his success, cites one factor that causes pastors to resist decisive but risky confrontation: "I'm still not comfortable about that situation. Even this morning I noticed the former Sunday school superintendent's car parked at the home of another fellow who recently quit coming to our church. That brought back all kinds of fears."

Afraid of another power struggle?

"Oh no. There's no power base in the church for them to work from now. Most people are genuinely pleased the way things turned out."

Then why is it still such a sore spot? Personal rejection? Fear of criticism?

"I think it's personal insecurity. I'm a pastor because I love people — and I guess I want to be loved in return. After Ralph and Martha resigned, I looked for a letter to the editor in our local newspaper. Seriously! Our situation has worked out beautifully; I did what had to be done for the health of this church. But I hope I never have to go through that again."

Youth and Inexperience

Reluctance also arises from lack of experience. Like most leadership skills, risk taking is learned on the job. Some experience lessens the fear. One pastor used the following analogy:

"When an airliner goes down and two hundred people are killed, statistics show that the number of people flying immediately falls off and stays off for three or four weeks, until the shock lessens and traffic gradually builds back up. The ones who cancel trips are the occasional flyers who probably don't know, or believe, the statistics on how safe flying is. Business people who fly all the time don't miss a trip.

"In many ways, a young pastor is like the infrequent flyer. He comes into a church with an underdeveloped ability to measure the risk of certain decisions."

Pastor Monitor put it this way: "This is my first church. For five years prior to coming here I was associate pastor and youth director of another church. In that position I was not accustomed to risks. I was sheltered by my senior pastor, at least from the emotional intensity. He ran interference for me more than once. I was not anxious for confrontation nor ready for the challenge I was about to face."

The veteran pastor, on the other hand, has learned that risky decisions are a natural part of ministry. The old hand realizes, *Although it may be unpleasant at times, on the whole the ministry is a safe place, and I'm going to survive the rough spots.*

The Unique Role of Pastor

The role of pastor is a delicate one, which also makes risk taking precarious.

Consider the difference between scientists and leaders. The scientist can study, perform experiments, and tell us whether a trip to the moon is possible. The leader, however, must say whether we ought to risk the human lives and invest the necessary funds. The scientist can provide the statistical probabilities, but someone else decides whether it *should* be done.

For the local church pastor, the roles of scientist and leader are rolled into one. As "scientist," the pastor researches and quantifies the risk. As "leader," the pastor decides whether the risk is consistent with the goals of the church. At times even a high probability of success is not enough to tip the scales in favor of making a certain decision. Perhaps the expense in terms of spiritual integrity or church morale is too great.

Colorado pastor Alan Ahlgrim uses an analogy to describe the multifaceted role pastors play: "A pastor wears many hats. One is the hat of the theologian. When I wear this hat, I make decisions based upon correct theology. A second is a shepherd's hat. My concern is the lost sheep, and I make decisions based on their welfare, indifferent to the rest. A third hat is for the administrator, when I must disregard the lost sheep and cater to the ninety and nine.

"I find the multiple-hat problem most acute in relating to staff and the core people of my congregation. How are they to know when I'm wearing the hat of friend and when I'm wearing the hat of administrator or theologian? I've found they can't. Some meetings I change hats so quickly that I come across as arbitrary or inconsistent. In my own mind I'm following perfect logic. To them I'm a scatterbrain, or worse.

"One of the most unfortunate problems this created was with a church secretary, one of the sweetest people I have ever known. She had the gifts of hospitality and mercy par excellence. She protected me from interruption during my study hours. She screened telephone calls. She even kept an eye on my health.

"Unfortunately, Brenda was not an efficient secretary for a large church. She became rattled easily. She confused phone messages and made frequent typing errors. She even listed people in the bulletin as having birthdays and anniversaries when in fact they had died a year ago. I knew something had to be done. After she made a series of serious errors with my correspondence, I finally said, 'This just isn't working out.' She said, 'Do you want me to resign?' I didn't answer her directly because as a gentle friend I wanted to let her have time to make the decision.

"I knew if she went home and finally decided to resign it would be devastating to her. So I called her husband, who was also my friend, and said, 'I think you should be aware of what happened this afternoon, because Brenda will need a lot of support.'

"He said, 'What you're telling me is you want her to resign.'

"I said yes, and as soon as I said it, I realized our friendship was over. Both of them were extraordinarily angry.

"Looking back, I should have told her I was firing her instead of trying to finesse her resignation. I thought I was taking a pastoral, humane approach. But I didn't realize that when one is wearing the administrative hat, the hat of pastor simply can't be seen. Unless you know the difference, a few bad experiences like this can paralyze you with indecision."

Shooting at a Moving Target

The decision whether to take a risk often depends on the importance of the issue. One pastor called this the "Choose Wisely the Cross You're Going to Die Upon" Decision.

One pastor made such a decision:

"From what I understand, one man in our congregation was ready to leave the church anyway. But when I came, I gave him the reason to do so.

"He had the belief that you should not eat in the church building. He felt it was a theological issue, based on 1 Corinthians 11, where Paul deals with abuses of Communion and the love feast. Since these good practices had apparently degenerated into drunkenness and gluttony, Paul suggests people should eat *before* they come to church so they don't defile God's house.

"I didn't think this should be taken as an across-the-board prohibition against eating at church. But this man felt strongly about it, and before I came he had somehow convinced the board they should prohibit eating in the church. Talking to others on the board, I discovered no one else felt strongly about it either way, so I decided to set my brother straight.

"I blithely assumed it would be a simple thing to go over to his house, explain the biblical principle, and correct his faulty interpretation. Once he understood how he had misconstrued the passage, the whole thing would work out.

"So I did, but it didn't. He got upset and left the church, and bad feelings always accompany that. Looking back, I should have kept my mouth shut for at least two years. Even then, I'm not sure I would have fought about this issue."

Complicating decisions like this is the fact that many issues change in importance from decade to decade. Thus, some reluctance to take risks comes from being uncertain whether this one is currently worth it. However, many issues in local-church ministry have always been with us. People don't change, and many of the confrontations pastors face are simply people problems.

Similar patterns punctuate the history of the church. Some of the problems facing the New Testament church (the question of circumcision, for example) are generally moot points for the modern church. There's no more risk in them. But overall risk has not lessened; only the specific risks have changed.

For example, an accelerated growth rate has made change itself a problem for the modern church leader. The successful church leader is one who can quickly discern changes and adjust leadership style accordingly: "We need to teach survival skills to cope with risk, uncertainty, and stress which will be difficult for us to manage as individuals and as society. . . . Education of this sort must be perceived as a lifelong process."[3]

Ever-changing conditions demand courageous, resourceful leaders. Gone are the days of a monolithic approach to decision making that fails to recognize that different procedures for decision making apply in different situations. Coping means flexibility where possible. Lynne Dixon, pastor of the Saratoga (Indiana) Church of God, used one approach in this case:

"I usually ask myself, 'Is this decision good for the church's organization and efficiency, or is it good for the church's maturity and the growth of the body of Christ? If it's mainly for efficiency, I tend to choose for the individual — we can be very inefficient at times.

"Our piano player is an example. She was an excellent musician at one time, but developed arthritis in her hands and also began losing her sense of timing. When it was time for the offertory, she would start playing when the plates were coming back in. But she did the best she could.

"Some people didn't like it, but they couldn't play the piano at all. This woman could, and she was willing to play even though it hurt a great deal. It might have been more efficient to look for another piano player, but there were none in our congregation, and it would have cost money to hire one from outside. I decided to stick with what we had. Maybe we didn't sound as good as other churches, but I didn't think that was quite as important."

To what lengths would she go to retain this pianist's right to minister at the expense of the "efficiency" of morning worship?

"If another pianist were available and willing, I think we'd change. If she still said, 'This is my ministry, and I won't give it up,' then I think I'd work at it, maybe by saying, 'Well, we need to develop some young pianists. Would you help me do that?' But for now, she's the best we have and doing the best she can."

Has this pastor ever had to decide for the group against the individual?

"Yes, when we purchased the vacant lot next to the church, several people in the church didn't think we ought to buy it. The majority did, though, so we went ahead with the purchase.

"I encouraged those who disagreed to come to all our meetings and voice their objections but to abide by the majority's wishes. After the eventual vote, they were upset, but no one left the church over it.

"In that case, it didn't seem to me the growth and maturity

of some individuals were at stake as much as it was just a difference of opinion over a business deal. The will of the majority was the deciding factor in that case. In a sense we went with the efficiency of the organization."

Clearly, the decision about when to take a risk is a complicated one. Many initial, innate fears tangle the decision. One way to overcome the uncertainty and conflicting value scales is to collect as much information as possible about the conditions of each case. Four questions cry for answers:

— What kind of risk is it?
— How important is it?
— What are the circumstances?
— What can I handle?

The first question is overlooked most often. Treating all decisions as the same type is to court disaster. To stress the importance of this distinction, the next six chapters provide guidelines for distinguishing different kinds of decisions. The last three questions are dealt with in chapters 10, 11, and 12.

Once these four questions are properly answered, it's easier to assess the riskiness of the situation and decide whether it is time to boldly step forth or wisely mark time.

FOUR

WHAT KIND OF RISK IS IT?

Security is the mother of danger and the grandmother of destruction.

THOMAS FULLER

Ignoring risk can be fatal.

Misunderstanding the risks of ministry, if not fatal, at least leads to ineptitude and failure. Misunderstanding, in this case, means treating all risks as if they were the same, a mistake that greatly increases the chances of disaster. So first we must identify the nature of the risk in question.

A primary resource, of course, is Scripture. Although the Bible never uses the word *risk*, story after story tells of risks taken, risks that end in flaming disasters or inspiring victories. Principles emerge from these stories.

Fred Craddock, professor of preaching and New Testament at Candler School of Theology, tells of a sermon he preached early in his ministry based on Luke 15, the story of the shepherd and the sheep. Craddock says he used to preach the sermon as if the shepherd left the ninety and nine in the safety of the fold and went out to search for the one lost sheep. After many years of telling this story with that presupposition, he discovered, to his embarrassment, that the text doesn't say that at all. The ninety-nine were left not in the safety of the fold but in the wilderness.

"That is far more descriptive of our heavenly Father," says

Craddock. "Only God, exhibiting his risky, careless love, would leave the ninety-nine in the wilderness to look for the one who is lost."[1] The principle: Risks taken with the goal of presenting the gospel to those who have not heard are high-priority risks indeed.

Look for risk in the New Testament and you find it. In fact, you find many different kinds of risk. Eventually categories emerge that help us develop other principles for making decisions in risky church situations.

The four general categories of problems the early church faced are ones we face today: theological, institutional, interpersonal, and personal. Although these categories are not mutually exclusive, they do make convenient hooks on which to hang different kinds of risks and the way we treat them.

Theological Risks

The most important category involves decisions that deal with fundamental theological truth. Perhaps the prime New Testament example is the Jerusalem Council in Acts 15. Some people had been teaching young Christians that circumcision was necessary for salvation. Other teachers, including Paul and Barnabas, realized this was a fundamental theological error — one that could not be tolerated no matter what fallout resulted from the confrontation.

At the meeting of apostles and elders to consider the question, Paul and Barnabas put their previous ministry on the line as evidence they were right. Had the council determined the other teachers were correct, Paul and Barnabas's future as teachers would have been shaky indeed.

We now know the council decided in favor of their theology and sent Paul and Barnabas to deliver a letter outlining the decision to the confused churches. Having stood for this theology, the church leaders now faced the risk that the young churches teaching this error would reject the edict and break away. Since the Christian church was young and vulnerable, the prospect of losing any new groups was frightening. Yet the theological principle at stake — the universality of the gospel — was so crucial that the risk had to be taken, regardless of the potential fallout.

In this case, the risk paid off. The one church we read about, the young Gentile congregation in Antioch, accepted the teaching with enthusiasm and remained healthy. Possibly there was some backlash not included in the text — perhaps a few members fell away — but the essential integrity of the body of Christ was insured.

Institutional Risks

Though the most important risks are theological, two-thirds of the risks a local church leader takes have little to do with theology. In fact, according to our survey, a full one-third of the risks a pastor takes fall into a category we call *institutional*. Just keeping the institutional church together and smoothly functioning makes up a considerable part of the local church leader's task.

Many institutional issues faced the New Testament church. In Acts 6 we find the dramatic growth and increasing ethnic diversity of the young church creating institutional problems. The Grecian Jews complained that their widows were being shortchanged in the daily distribution of food in favor of the widows of the Aramaic-speaking Christians.

The Twelve realized that administering this benevolence was an important practical issue but in a different category from the task of preaching the Word. They met and decided that "it would not be right for us to neglect the ministry of the word of God in order to wait on tables." So they asked the church to select seven wise and spiritual men to be assigned the task of dividing up the food fairly.

The whole church was pleased with the solution. An unfair and potentially divisive situation was confronted directly, and the risk of schism was avoided simply by delegating the problem to a group of people with the gifts to solve such problems.

The institutional issue was not ignored, nor was it allowed to deflect the church from its primary mission of spreading the Good News.

Interpersonal Risks

A third category involves interpersonal disagreement among church members. Because human nature is universal, many New Testament examples of interpersonal conflict could just as easily have been written last week as two thousand years ago. For example, 1 Corinthians 6 warns believers against taking a dispute with another believer before secular judges, certainly a continuing concern in our litigious society.

Equally familiar is the human nature displayed in Jesus' parable of the unmerciful servant. In the story, a king was calling in outstanding debts from his servants. One servant owed a huge sum and was unable to pay. The king was going to sell the servant and his family into slavery to recoup some of his losses. The servant begged for rescission of the obligation. The king felt sorry for him and forgave the debt.

The parable has a bittersweet ending, however. The servant also had some outstanding debts. And when he faced one of his debtors, a fellow servant who couldn't pay, the forgiven servant refused to forgive.

When the king heard about this hardness of heart, he threw the servant in jail and berated him: "You wicked servant. I canceled all that debt of yours because you begged me to. Shouldn't you have had mercy on your fellow servant just as I had on you?"

The king was well within his legal rights to demand the debt. Since his kingdom didn't depend on recovery of the money, however, he was also well within his rights to cancel the debt.

The root issue here was an interpersonal one — how the first servant related to the second servant.

Personal Risks

Some risks that church leaders take can only be described as personal — involving their call to ministry or personal relationships. Sometimes a relationship problem is based on theological, institutional, or interpersonal concerns. Sometimes, however, the crisis is essentially personal in nature. Personal crises take several forms.

The call to ministry. The call has changed somewhat since New Testament times. In Acts 1, for example, Matthias was added to the eleven apostles as a result of drawing lots. Although many young people today "put out a fleece" to decide whether to go into the ministry, few flip a coin to make the decision. We take a more "professional" approach.

In addition, after a pastor has been in a church for a year, or five, or ten, sometimes his or her ministry gifts no longer match those required by the congregation. The risky question: Should I stay or leave?

Personal growth or stagnation. Pastors also face decisions regarding their personal spiritual growth. I suspect the apostle Paul would have died a thousand deaths in a denominational desk job. The "great lion of God" seemed to thrive on the missionary tasks God set before him. Paul decided how to use his gifts by listening to God, not weighing the opportunities elsewhere. The question: How can I use my gifts to the kingdom's greatest advantage?

Personal conflicts. In cases of personal conflict with members of the congregation, the burden usually falls on the church leader to resolve the problem. And rightly so.

In some cases, however, this is simply not possible. Occasionally, the pastor's spiritual batteries are too low to turn the other cheek or go the extra mile. Sometimes the situation has deteriorated beyond what two people, however well-intentioned, can patch up. In those cases, the best resource is the elders, who can help provide the outside objectivity needed.

Sometimes the conflict is with a staff member. Paul and

Barnabas had barely gotten into their first missionary journey when they had a "sharp disagreement about whether to take Mark along with them" (Acts 15:36ff.). They resolved the conflict by dividing their energies, Barnabas taking Mark with him, and Paul finding a new associate missionary in Silas. Apparently the arrangement worked very well.

When to Take a Risk?

Not every situation, of course, calls for risky action. Some call for maintenance, some for compromise, others for careful and premeditated ignoring. Yet more serious situations develop from a pastor failing to take action than from acting too hastily.

How to know when to rush in where angels fear to tread? The first step is to identify what kind of problem you're dealing with. Attempting to handle an interpersonal problem as if it were an institutional issue only compounds the problem. Similarly, a theological misunderstanding must be dealt with much differently than a personal crisis.

In the next four chapters we will discuss the four kinds of risk in more detail, outlining specifically the approach to be taken in each.

FIVE

THEOLOGICAL RISKS

Obedience is the organ of spiritual knowledge.

FREDERICK ROBERTSON

T

he most important risks are theological. Almost every pastor will at some time take a risk because of an issue of theology. One pastor reported the following account:

"A pregnant girl and her boyfriend wanted me to marry them. She didn't attend church regularly, although she was a member. I had baptized her several years previously, and that was her rationale for wanting me to marry them: 'I was baptized here, and I'd like to be married here.'

"When I talked with them about their relationship and lifestyle, neither of them considered God an important influence. I told them that with that attitude I couldn't do the ceremony.

"Usually when I face a risky decision, I consult the elders. In this case, though, I felt I couldn't because the young woman's situation was not common knowledge. These situations put a pastor in a tough position. You have private knowledge, make a decision based on that knowledge, and then people criticize your decision without knowing all the facts. That's when you find out your true mettle: are you willing to do what must be done to maintain the theological integrity of the church?"

In our survey of local-church leaders, we learned that on the average, pastors make one or two significant theological stands per year (see Chart 1). Issues run the gamut from questions about the deity of Christ to the mission of the church.

One pastor remembers a conflict with the treasurer and two other people who wished to do away with the missions program: "To cut out mission work is to cut the life line of the church. Matthew 28:18–20 clearly teaches this. When I fought the move to end mission involvement, those who disagreed tried to get me to vacate the pulpit. Eventually this small faction left the church. We are now doing well again."

When a stand is taken on such an important issue, the results again and again prove the wisdom of the confrontation. This pastor saw positive results:

"The renewed commitment to missions brought the body of Christ together. The people in the congregation respect me as their leader more, and I sense they are deeper spiritually."

Church leaders, regardless of polity and theology, become dead serious about core beliefs — serious enough not to allow for compromise. For some, the extent of those core beliefs is broad, for others, more narrow. But all have theological standards. When those standards are challenged, leaders face some of the most difficult times in their ministries. Sometimes the resulting disagreement ends amicably. If both sides evidence spiritual maturity, discussion can take place. Then, if a resolution cannot be worked out, a peaceful parting of the ways is possible.

At other times, however, theological disagreements severely damage or divide congregations. The authority of Scripture, gifts of the Spirit, euthanasia, and abortion are a few examples.

The Bible chronicles many instances of spiritual warriors who have gone to battle for the integrity of the gospel. When Paul realized Peter was requiring Gentile Christians to follow Jewish customs, he confronted him and pointed out that Gentile sinners are not "justified by observing the law but by faith in Jesus Christ" (Gal. 2:11ff.). In modern terms this is analo-

CHART 1

TOUGH PASTORAL DECISIONS: HOW MANY?

The bars here depict that on average, pastors say they make:
— between one and two tough THEOLOGICAL DECISIONS each year
— between one and two tough INSTITUTIONAL DECISIONS each year
— between one and two tough INTERPERSONAL DECISIONS each year.

On later charts, survey responses will be divided into two groups: pastors who have been forced to leave a church and those who haven't. Our research shows more variation between the two groups in the number and type of decisions made each year.

The most obvious observation from this chart is that not all decisions are theological rulings. In any given year, apparently, the major questions and disputes that arise are evenly divided between the theological, institutional, and interpersonal categories.

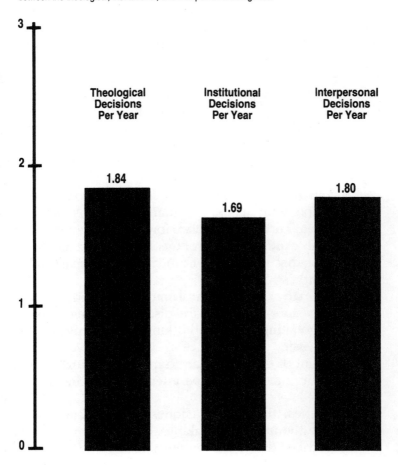

gous to a missionary pointing out his denominational superior's misunderstanding of theology. It is not always good for advancement, but when a legitimate point of theology is at stake, the risk must be taken.

Needless to say, not every issue warrants this kind of do-or-die action. One pastor put it this way: "When you really come down to it, many of our decisions are based not on the theological correctness of the situation but on what our people will respond to. Is that always wrong? Not when you're making a decision like, 'Should we hold our annual skating party at the Skateaway or the Skate & Dolly?' It's wrong when a theological tenet is at stake. In the first case, the good of the many supercedes the preference of the few. In the second case, correct theology supercedes even the wish of the majority."

Great caution must be taken in identifying a conflict as theological. Many nontheological disagreements get labeled as theological: whether to use plastic or glass Communion cups, the brand of the Communion bread, the presence of altar flowers. Each can be falsely billed as an intricate and essential point of theology.

Our survey results revealed that pastors who reported making more than the average two theological decisions per year did so at great danger. There is a direct correlation between pastors who make more than two "theological" decisions per year and those who are forced to leave their church (see Chart 2). Finding a point of theology hidden under every altar-flower discussion can be hazardous to pastoral and church health.

Why are many nontheological matters branded as theological? Some pastors use theological discussion to avoid the hard work of negotiating tough institutional and interpersonal conflicts. It is easier to pronounce an issue "answered" by an obscure point of theology than to moderate a turf battle between the Sunday school superintendent and the girls' club director.

Some issues, though, can honestly be classified several ways. Take the issue of drinking alcoholic beverages. One pastor described this as the toughest decision he had made in

CHART 2

PASTORAL CASUALTIES
AND THEOLOGICAL DECISIONS

The bars here compare the two groups of respondents, Fired and Not Fired, according to the number of theological decisions they say they make per year.

The Not Fired group is more aware than the Fired group that one or two theological issues a year will come up that need a pastoral decision. Fewer of them than the Fired group claimed to make no theological decisions per year. Also, fewer of the Not Fired group were likely to misread other types of decisions as theological. The more theological decisions made per year, the greater the chance of being fired.

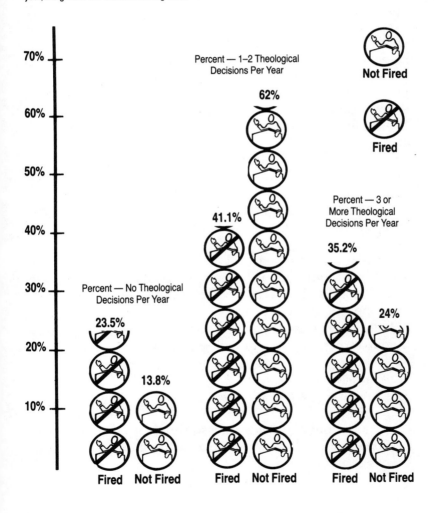

ministry, but he classified it as an institutional issue, not a theological one. "I had to reaffirm the stance of our movement that church leaders, but not necessarily church members, practice total abstinence from alcoholic beverages. This has always been our denominational position, but in the local churches some leaders were involved in drinking. The denominational line had to be drawn."

Another pastor, however, defended the same issue in theological terms: "I felt the Bible condoned the use of alcohol in moderation, but my church felt total abstinence was God honoring and biblically based. As a result I was not accepted as the pastor. I was told that even if I personally abstained but taught that moderation was permissible, I could not be recommended to any church in my denomination."

Issues have varying degrees of theological impact. The important principle, however, is that not all disputes are theologically based. Our survey respondents said only one-third of the difficult decisions they make in a year concern theological issues.

Identifying that one-third, however, is key. The following three questions help determine whether a situation is truly theological:

1. Does this situation threaten a core belief of our church? Or is it a peripheral issue that allows for some difference of position?

2. If left unaddressed, will theological precedent be established that could lead to long-term weakening of our commitment? Or is it simply a reflection of some spiritual immaturity that time and love will remedy?

3. Is the issue purely one of theology? Or is theology being used to camouflage a nontheological problem?

The Principle:
The Law of Right and Wrong

Once identified, theological issues call for vigorous action. Left unattended, they can destroy a church by snapping its unifying thread.

Theological risks are taken according to the "law of right and wrong." The objective — theological purity — admits no compromise. Resolution need not be blunt or hasty, but the risk to achieve the right must be taken regardless.

Following the law of right and wrong is not a simple matter, however. The decision, the goal, may be clear, but how to achieve that goal with the fewest casualties may not be as obvious. One pastor recalls: "I made a decision, based on my understanding of 1 Timothy 3, that prospective officers must be men who had not been divorced. Several nominees were disqualified because they did not meet this standard. As a result, they and their friends and families grew hostile. A few who were disqualified could not be reconciled, and hostility hardened against me. Looking back I would not have changed the standards for officers; I still believe they were biblical. But I would have handled the disqualifications in a more personal, loving manner."

Occasionally the theological issue itself needs to be redefined by an overriding principle of love. One pastor remembered a particularly difficult problem: "I was asked to baptize a young adult who was extremely afraid of water. So intense was the phobia that the young man couldn't even take a shower; he had to take sponge baths. Our church practices baptism by immersion. This candidate wanted me to perform the baptism in our church. But because of his fear of water, the only way to do it was by sprinkling. The church board and I struggled with many questions about doing a baptism by sprinkling, considering the theological beliefs of our denomination. For a time the church board was split. Finally we voted to sprinkle the young man in a private service."

The law of right and wrong needs to be followed, not harshly, but in accord with God's law of love.

The Motivation:
Christian Obedience

Obedience cannot be understood without understanding the standard by which it is measured. For *Christian* obedience, the standard is not first of all a list of ethical or moral laws (though those have their place). The standard is God's will for us. Christian obedience asks us to do what God says even though it may be something we would never have thought of doing.

Jean-Pierre de Caussade said in *The Sacrament of the Present Moment*: "All saints become saints by fulfilling those duties themselves to which they have been called. It is not by the things they do, their nature, or particular qualities that holiness must be judged. It is obeying those orders which sanctify souls and enlightens, purifies and humbles them."[1]

The call to obedience, paradoxically, is the most important principle we live by but also one of the most restricted.

It is the most important because all the ultimate questions of life and faith are answered by the criterion of obedience. Is this something God wants us to do? Is this part of God's plan for our church? Deuteronomy 11:26–28 summarizes the principle: "Obey and you will be blessed. Disobey and you will be cursed."

Yet the nature of obedience, when dealing with the ultimate, also restricts it. Ultimate principles can be applied only to ultimate questions. For questions of less-than-ultimate value, obedience as practiced by less-than-perfect human beings in a less-than-perfect world can be inappropriate, even dangerous. On many issues we simply don't have direct commands from God to obey and are left to sanctified common sense. The great temptation is to obey human ideas, mistaking them for God's.

The danger of disobedience to God's clear commands, of course, is rebellion and spiritual death. But we often overzealously try to apply the principle of obedience to problems that are not ultimate or theological in nature. Strange things happen when we confuse institutional, interpersonal, and personal situations with theological ones and apply the motivation of obedience to them all.

When we confuse theological problems with institutional ones. Acts 5:29 tells us we're "to obey God rather than men." But obedience can become a gun in the hands of the authoritarian figure. Demanding blind obedience to *human* ideas, leaders, and institutions can lead to fanaticism and cultism.

Needless to say, there is an appropriate "obedience" toward authorities or church leaders. However, it shouldn't be confused with the kind of obedience we express toward God. Since in local church decision-making situations it's important to distinguish between the obedience we show to God and the appropriate respect due to our human leaders, perhaps *commitment* is a better word than *obedience* to describe what we're after in institutional issues. This idea will be developed in the next chapter.

Blind obedience to human institutions inevitably weakens the institution. If church harmony is built on the principle of obedience to a constitution, then any crisis that arises becomes an institution-threatening situation. Christian obedience was not intended as a handy fire extinguisher for disagreement in the church. As we shall see in chapter 6, there is a better principle for solving institutional problems.

When we confuse theological problems with interpersonal ones. Indiscriminate use of obedience in interpersonal situations can lead to inhumanity. Psychologist Stanley Milgram illustrated this in a classic series of experiments done in the early 1960s. Volunteers from all walks of life participated in a study described to them as an experiment in memory and learning. They were asked to administer electric shocks to people during the experiment. Over 60 percent of the people pressed the electric shock button and continued to do so even when they heard shouts of pain from the victims. The volunteers were prompted by psychologists in white lab coats who said, "The experiment requires that you continue."[2]

Where mere obedience is used as the criterion for determining interpersonal relationships, varying levels of inhumanity result. The church is not exempt from this danger. We are called to reprove our brothers and sisters to keep our doctrine and beliefs pure, but we are also called to do so in love and forgiveness. As soon as we begin to see ourselves (rather than

God) as the repository of all theological truth, we lose sight of our own fallibility, and arrogance and ruthlessness, in the name of God's work, can result.

Are We Capable of Discernment?

How difficult is it to apply the principle of obedience to our relationship with God, and fashion a more realistic principle in our other relationships? Perhaps not as difficult as we may think.

Psychologists David Bock and Neil Warren did a study aimed at determining the link between religious belief and interpersonal relationships. By using a belief scale, they identified three different groups of people: nonreligious, moderately religious, and very religious. They then ran those three different groups through an experiment similar to Milgram's.

The experimenters expected to find that the very religious, because of their extreme sense of obedience to God and theological principles, would also exhibit a high degree of obedience to the authoritative experimenters — the doctors and psychologists. They discovered the *opposite*. The moderately religious and nonreligious were far more eager to administer shocks to the experimental subjects.

Bock and Warren concluded that men and women who are undecided about basic religious issues are less able to be decisive when confronted by an ethical dilemma. They tend to forfeit their choice to any convenient authority figure. On the other hand, those who adopt definite religious stances (*including* obedience to God) are more able to act in accordance with ethical values of love and justice.[3]

A commitment to obey God alone does not inhibit a person's ability to distinguish between the various kinds of risks. In fact, it may very well give more clarity of insight.

Conclusion

What does this mean in the local church? It means that if we intend to decide a question on the basis of obedience to the theological canons of right and wrong, we need to be sure we're dealing with a theological question. Answers to the question of what is theological will vary from person to person (even though we agree there are "irreducible minimums"). But the decision is an all-important one, because our survey clearly showed the more things a pastor identifies as theological, the more risk he or she incurs. The decision determines the approach we take, and wise discernment can prevent costly mistakes.

SIX

INSTITUTIONAL RISKS

That which is necessary is never a risk.

CARDINAL DE RETZ

Institutional decisions risk the health of the organization. They may involve finances, facilities, or personnel, but their common denominator is that if ignored, the institution will fragment, go bankrupt, suffer serious decline, or fail to realize its full potential.

Perhaps the toughest of these decisions is related to personnel, particularly when a staff member must be fired. There's risk in letting someone go. Drexel Rankin, minister of Carmel (Indiana) Christian Church, remembers firing an organist: "He possessed remarkable talent, but he was undependable. Occasionally he would show up fifteen minutes late for Sunday morning worship; I would already have winged a prelude and played the first hymn when he would walk in. After he did that the third time, I told him, 'Don't ever do that again. If you do, don't bother coming!'

"Then at the Easter sunrise service, he didn't show at all. No word from him. I tried calling him at home but got no answer. I found out a couple of days later that he had been at the hospital. He had evidently hurt a finger and gone to the emergency room, but he didn't bother to call anybody. He just skipped the service.

"I was angry. I told the moderator of our church council I

was firing the organist. The moderator liked the organist and didn't want him to be fired, so he took it to the church council, questioning my judgment in firing the organist. I was in the frying pan that night. But I believed in what I was doing. I told the council the whole story, how angry I was, and that I was sticking by my decision. It went down hard, but they finally agreed.

"Afterwards, I realized I should have brought the decision to the council first, and should have dealt with the organist after my anger had cooled. I learned my lesson. It was good I did, because a couple of years later I faced the same situation with our choir director.

"She also had talent galore. She was a fine person, and everyone loved her, but she was disorganized, undependable, and frequently late. I'd sit down with her and say, 'What's going on? Why are you showing up late to rehearsal? Can I help you work this out?'

"But our discussions didn't seem to help. She began to talk about resigning. Morale began to suffer. After she missed three staff meetings in a row, I knew I had to act. I managed to get her to come to the office. She said she could stay only five minutes: 'We're not going to be able to talk until late next week. I just haven't got the time.'

"I said, 'Diane, that's not acceptable.'

"She said again, 'Well, I've been thinking about resigning anyway.'

"At that point she had said it once too often, and I said, 'I think you ought to write it out and lay it on my desk Sunday.' That was a far healthier situation than my firing her. Positive resolutions can sometimes be arrived at if you show patience and use confrontation skills. Even better is learning to rely on the church council for guidance in sticky personnel matters."

Not every institutional crisis is a personnel problem. It may be a financial mutiny by members who withhold their tithe as a means of forcing their will on the rest of the body. It may be trying to reconcile your church's interests with those of the denomination. Sometimes it is the agonizing decision about whether to build a new building.

The first step in identifying an institutional problem is to make sure it is not theological (see the questions suggested in the previous chapter). Then ask the following:

1. If left unattended, will this crisis damage the organizational viability of our church?

2. Are the theological or personal issues raised really germane to the discussion? Or are they red herrings, distracting from the institutional issue?

3. Am I, as pastor or church leader, the cause of the conflict? If I were not here, would there still be a conflict? (This identifies whether the situation is interpersonal or personal rather than institutional).

The Principle:
The Law of the Good of the Many

Institutional decisions differ from theological ones in that democratic rather than theocratic principles apply.

Church institutions provide the venue for the proclamation of the gospel. They are the context for discipleship, the staging area for evangelization. The church structure does not do the proclaiming, discipling, or evangelizing, but it allows these important purposes to be fulfilled.

The structure, then, does not have the enduring value that theological truth has. It is temporary and utilitarian. If the structure fails to meet the spiritual needs of the people, it fails its purpose and must be changed. For example, if people in a particular cultural setting can meet together only in the evenings, then the church should hold services in the evening.

Thus, many legitimate church structures are possible. When you make effective presentation of Christian principles the goal, flexibility becomes essential. The institutional church is the horse upon which the rider bound for glory rides. It needs to be a strong horse, but whether it's a palomino or a black stallion makes little difference; it may even take a relay of horses to get there.

Albert Schweitzer took on the almost-impossible task of establishing a modern hospital in a remote part of Africa. His eventual success was due in large measure to his willingness to be flexible. Hospitals are infamous for inflexible rules, yet Dr. Schweitzer broke almost all the Western taboos in order to meet the special needs of interior Africa. The result: a hospital that worked, without sacrificing any *essential* medical principles.

One of his biographers, George Marshall, notes: "The Schweitzer Hospital is unlike any other in the United States or Europe. Growing out of the flexible working philosophy of Dr. Schweitzer as he blended his knowledge of medical needs with the culture of the African, it is also unique among African hospitals. . . . The justification of the unique Schweitzer Hospital, plain and simple, is that it has worked."[1]

In deciding an institutional issue, then, the pastor tries to determine which alternative will serve the largest number of people. That is, what will allow 100 percent of the congregation to worship and serve God most effectively? In difficult situations, of course, 100-percent solutions may be impossible. Many decisions will satisfy only 90 percent; some only 60 or 70 percent. Truly agonizing decisions arise occasionally when the congregation is split evenly.

Institutional decisions can often be no-win situations. Our research showed little correlation between making or not making these decisions and staying or leaving (see Chart 3). Ministries may be forfeited either way. These are the truly selfless decisions, done for the good of the body, though recognition may not come for years, if ever.

One pastor remembered such a situation: "The board chairman and the financial secretary constituted the power structure of this Congregational church. By the middle of my second year, I realized change was needed for the congregation to survive. These two men fought any action by members or by me. For example, the board chairman questioned my purchasing power. He said I could buy only one thing in the next year, a new typewriter. I called his threatening bluff by stating the procedure called for in the church constitution — presenting written requests to the entire board. I then asked

CHART 3

PASTORAL CASUALTIES AND INSTITUTIONAL DECISIONS

The bars here compare the two groups of respondents, Fired and Not Fired, according to the number of institutional decisions they say they make per year.

On institutional issues, pastors in the two groups make about the same number of decisions a year. But a few more of the Fired group fail to see that institutional decisions need to be made — saying they don't make any tough institutional decisions in a year. And a few more pastors from the Not Fired group are more active in institutional issues by making three or more decisions per year.

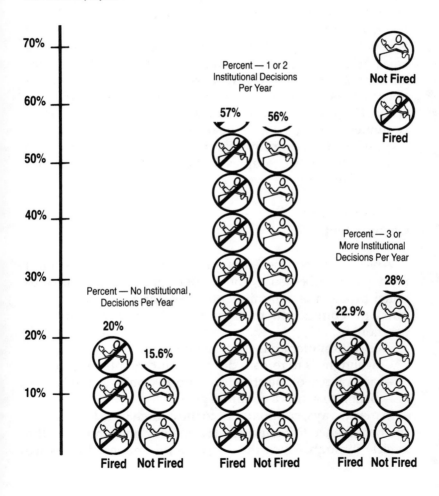

the board to clarify the procedure. This made him my enemy. Soon thereafter he presented a detailed list of my shortcomings. From then on, everything was a battle. I fought it over the next year and a half and "won" — the two leaders left the church. Eventually, though, I, too, left because the church needed healing after this protracted battle."

Of course, not all such decisions lead to the pastor leaving the church. One survey respondent noted, "Two couples started a home Bible study without church sanction. People from our church were invited as if it were church sanctioned. We had three problems with this. First, new church activities had to be approved by the board. For a Bible study, approval is usually automatic, but the procedure keeps us aware of small-group interaction. Second, it was organized to replace an existing program. Third, there was no control over the doctrinal teachings, and in this case, there was reason to be wary. The board asked the couple to stop the study. They continued, saying it was none of our business. So we spelled out the board's disapproval for those attending. Some left the church with the two couples, but the church as a whole has increased in unity."

The Motivation:
Commitment

Whereas the proper pastoral approach to a theological problem was obedience, the proper approach to an institutional problem is commitment. A pastor and congregation must be committed to their church for it to continue functioning.

This commitment has three dimensions:
— willingness to remain despite inducements to leave
— acceptance of the structure's norms, values, and beliefs
— action to achieve common goals.[2]

In many ways, commitment to the church is no less intense than obedience to Scripture. The institutional church is the vehicle through which the gospel is proclaimed. Just as we maintain the health of our vocal chords so we can speak and we service our automobiles so they can provide transportation, we maintain the structure and harmony of our churches so they can speak and embody the gospel. Indeed, in the eyes of the world, a pastor's commitment to the institutional church is every bit as odd, perhaps, as obedience to the Word.

Commitment, however, can lead to extremes. G. Gordon Liddy, the Watergate burglar, for example, confused commitment to a government with a devotion that should be shown only toward an absolute moral principle of God. Apathy, on the other hand, will ruin a religious institution.

Applying the principle of commitment properly means avoiding either extreme. When a pastor considers an institutional question, he or she must be willing to perform the hated, suspect act: *compromise*. Making an organization work in a fallen world means we must find the middle way between expecting a perfect City of God and settling for an earthly enterprise judged only by standards of money and members. It is often difficult for a theologically trained pastor to realize that compromise in *institutional* matters is appropriate and necessary.

In a recent interview Henry Kissinger was asked, "Why were you such a successful diplomat?"

"I think," said Kissinger, "it's because through my experience and study of world history, I realized that notions of clear-cut victory or unconditional surrender were illusory. The best settlement has no absolute victor or absolute loser. In world affairs the shortest distance between two points is often a labyrinth."

Such is the spirit a church leader must adopt in considering institutional risks.

Dangers

Just as applying the principle of obedience to every church decision leads to problems (outlined in the last chapter), so using the principle of commitment for situations other than institutional ones compounds their difficulty.

It is perhaps easiest to confuse an institutional problem with a theological one and ask for obedience when commitment is necessary. For example, when a leader claims, "God told me to build this building," he has masked an institutional matter — will a new building help our church be more effective, and can we afford it? — as a theological issue. Instead of asking people to commit themselves to the hard work of determining building needs and projecting income, he demands their obedience by divine fiat.

Why does this type of confusion occur? Partly because there *is* a relationship between theology and the institution. Good theology undergirds all decisions in a church, whether institutional, interpersonal, or personal. Good theology increases the chances that a church will be a good institution. In an intriguing study reported in the *Review of Religious Research* in 1977, Doyle Johnson investigated the relationship between commitment to the church and the acting out of justice in the community. He found those persons most likely to be racially tolerant and working for social good in the community were also the most involved and committed to the institutional church.[3]

Problems arise, however, when institutional decisions that call for a pragmatic answer are "solved" by demanding obedience. Demand obedience to a church *leader* on institutional matters, and cultic devotion usually results. Call for obedience to a *group* or institution, and chauvinism results. In institutional matters, discussion and give-and-take are needed, not unquestioning obedience.

In many ways, obedience is easier to give than commitment. What passes for obedience in the cases of cultism and chauvinism is often mindless escapism, the tired, panic-stricken obeisance of people unwilling to work out the complex problems of making an institution effective. *Let's let our leaders worry about this; we'll do whatever they say*, seems to be the attitude.

Commitment, on the other hand, calls for wrestling with

the tensions between the sacred and the profane, for doing deeds that defy the ethos of the age, and for persisting in the face of imperfect people and imperfect laws. At every stage we are tempted to throw it all over and say, *What's the use?* Commitment is a muscular word, a sinewy perseverance that calls for hard decisions and a willingness to take responsibility for making a church work. It expects high ideals yet relaxes about the inevitable slippages and restarts characteristic of a fallen world.

Institutional problems can also be confused with interpersonal problems. When that happens, a leader calls for forgiveness when commitment is needed. Take, for example, two elders fighting over whether a church should start a day school. Two church members are in conflict; it appears to be an interpersonal problem. But what is really at stake is an institutional matter — will a day school help this church serve its members and community more effectively? In this case, a pastor's primary task is to keep the parties discussing the difficult institutional decision until they reach resolution. The pastor's attitude must be "Let's commit ourselves to working this out."

But when the conflict becomes painful, it's tempting to give up and call for forgiveness: "This fight has been going on too long. Let's just let it drop. Jim and Larry, you both need to forgive each other." But spreading the balm of forgiveness without resolving the underlying institutional conflict heals nothing. It is like trying to cure a broken arm with petroleum jelly.

If a pastor confuses an institutional risk with an interpersonal one, the institution is weakened. There are times when a church does not need more forgiveness, or rhetoric about loving and caring, but simply a dogged, persistent attention to structure.

Dean Kelly in his book, *Why Conservative Churches Are Growing*, argues that liberal churches lack "strictness," while conservative churches exercise discipline more and take religion more seriously.[4] The result is stronger institutions, because conservatives are willing to weed out nonfunctioning members by applying the rule of the good of the many. They're willing to examine organizational and structural problems instead of ignoring them under the guise of pseudo-forgiveness.

Conclusion

Commitment balances between obedience to theological principle and humble forgiveness of one another. Perhaps this can best be illustrated by an example in church history. The story's hero is Cyprian, a wealthy, well-educated citizen of Carthage who became a powerful bishop in the early church because of his great administrative skills.

In A.D. 250, the church emerged from a period of intense persecution. Many Christians had apostatized — under threat of torture, sworn allegiance to the Roman emperor instead of God. When the persecution ended, many of the apostates wanted to rejoin the church. Theologians of the day took three different positions on whether that should be allowed.

At one extreme stood Cornelius. During the persecution, Cornelius had personally maintained his faith despite torture and great hardship. However, he wanted to apply blanket forgiveness to any apostates who asked to be restored.

At the other extreme stood Novatian, who felt that anyone who fell away had committed the unpardonable sin of blaspheming the Holy Spirit. Novatian considered the problem purely theological, with the law of right or wrong fully applicable.

Cyprian took a middle position. If the apostates wanted to come back, they should be allowed. But they should be required to go through certain disciplines in order to reestablish membership. Cyprian didn't deny the theological and interpersonal elements to the question, but he saw it primarily as an institutional issue — the integrity of church membership, the lifeblood of institutional harmony, was at stake. Apostasy couldn't be condoned by easy forgiveness; otherwise, why should anyone remain faithful under persecution? Yet those who wanted to return needed to be reincorporated.[5]

Cyprian faced one of the early church's first confrontations with what it meant for the church to be both a structured organization as well as a spiritual organism. In institutional matters, his decision is still a worthy model.

SEVEN

INTERPERSONAL RISKS

Nothing in this lost world bears the impress of the Son of God so surely as forgiveness.

ALICE CAREY

Many conflicts, from the sublime to the petty, fall under the category of *interpersonal*. At times pastors must referee parties disputing issues of significance for the entire congregation. One pastor described his involvement this way:

"Right now one of the elders, a powerful man, is angry about the way one of our young people dresses for Communion. The elder is angry almost to the point of leaving. Since we serve Communion every week, it is not just an occasional problem. The boy in question has been on the verge of rebellion for a couple of years. His parents are not pleased with some of his friends. They wish he would spend more time with the church youth group.

"One expression of his rebellion is his dress — jeans, T-shirt, long hair. I think the boy, by dressing the way he does, is asking the church, 'Am I acceptable to you, or do you want to put me in a tight box?' In my judgment, it is more important for us to say, 'Yes, you are acceptable,' than to enforce a tight dress code. That's the position I have taken.

"That position has created some fallout. This elder has had things pretty much his way for a long time. He may leave. I've taken steps to prevent that. I went to the father of the boy and said, 'Here's the situation, and this is the stand I've taken. Be aware that it is creating some hard feelings.' It's a way of asking him, when he hears his son criticized, to not lash out or overreact.

"I also had lunch with the elder. I told him this was the stand I'm taking because I want the church to send a good message to all the kids. I told him I knew he didn't agree with my decision. Then I said, 'Alex, what do you think God wants you to do in this situation?'

"I have also talked to the boy. I want him to know that although we are accepting him, his dress is the cause of controversy. His reaction is, 'This is the way kids dress. It's not immoral.' He's correct. But he's also immature. If he were twenty-eight, I wouldn't put up with it. But he's not.

"I don't know where this will end. The last couple of times he was served Communion, he wore a shirt with a collar. So it's improving. Had we cut him off, would he be growing?

"This is a difficult decision, the kind I hate most — calling people to responsibility. It's as if I'm pitting the comfort of one member against the comfort of another. How do you weigh something like that?"

Other times, pastors face interpersonal issues that can only be described as childish. One survey respondent wrote about a diaper controversy. A nursery worker refused to change a baby's diaper because the woman who brought the baby was not the mother — only a baby sitter. The worker felt a baby sitter should not bring a child to a church service and have someone else do her baby-sitting. Therefore, the worker refused to change the diaper.

The nursery supervisor disagreed and asked the worker to change the diaper. A fight ensued. They took the issue to the pastor, undoubtedly because his seminary training qualified him to arbitrate diaper controversies. When he decided in favor of the nursery supervisor, the furious nursery worker and her entire family, including two married daughters, left the church.

Petty does not mean less intense. Interpersonal conflicts can escalate no matter what the issue, pulling the leader's emotions into the mix.

One pastor remembers: "My toughest decision was confronting the music coordinator and his wife for not preparing Easter service music — after both of them had been informed. Their excuse? My wife had told them, but they wanted to hear it from me. And they never asked me. Since their son was a board member, this dispute easily could have cost me my job."

Another pastor wrote: "I recommended the church help a family pay for a funeral. This infuriated another family. They began a series of accusations regarding my competency and criticized me publicly. They called for my resignation. After a month or so I was forced to leave."

Because of their vitriolic nature, interpersonal conflicts require early pastoral action. One of the strongest correlations the survey revealed: the more interpersonal decisions a pastor makes, the more likely he or she is to remain at a church. Pastors who accurately identify the interpersonal base of problems, even when they are camouflaged by theological and institutional rationales, deal with risky situations most successfully (see Chart 4).

They not only spot the interpersonal dimensions, they confront them — head on and early. Writes one pastor: "Lately we've had a major lack of love here — biting comments, parking lot meetings, lost tempers at board meetings. I've been here nine years and have repeatedly taught love, reconciliation, and working out problems together. A few have heard, but most still want to whisper complaints and criticisms to committees while remaining safely anonymous. I would be a hypocrite if I didn't put my sermons into practice; also, when I put off confronting problems, I usually suffer mild depression. So I confronted the people involved, and already a great deal of healing has taken place."

Interpersonal conflict can be most destructive — and most surprising, since the precipitating issues can range so widely.

CHART 4

PASTORAL CASUALTIES
AND INTERPERSONAL DECISIONS

The bars here compare the two groups of respondents, Fired and Not Fired, according to the number of interpersonal decisions they say they make per year.

The Not Fired group is much more aware than the Fired group that many of the tough issues a pastor faces are interpersonal questions rather than theological. Fewer of the Not Fired group say they make no interpersonal decisions per year, and many more of them make three or more interpersonal decisions a year.

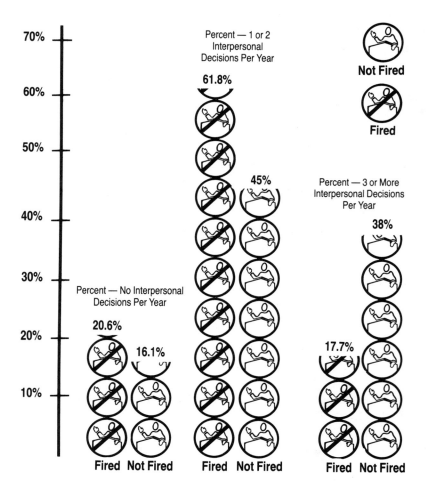

That's why it is crucial to correctly identify an interpersonal conflict. Questions to help make that identification:

1. Are you certain there is no real theological issue at stake? The questions in chapter 5 help answer this.

2. Eliminate the institutional possibility by asking, "What is the worst that could happen if this problem would escalate drastically?" If the answer is "One of the parties might leave the church (even taking a *few* others with them), yet the church would probably recover its health rather quickly," then the issue is most likely interpersonal. This doesn't mean the problem is any less important than a theological or institutional one. It simply means we deal with it in a different way.

3. Can I go the extra mile (in counseling time and tolerating inappropriate behavior) with these people without endangering the church as a whole?

4. What is my motivation in giving extra time and tolerance to this person or persons? Ask this question to make sure your involvement isn't fueled by inappropriate personal concerns.

In a sense, interpersonal problems move beyond both theological and institutional ones. They are truly matters of pastoral care. Apollodorus was a loyal disciple of Socrates. When Socrates ran afoul of the Athenian government and was sentenced to death on trumped-up charges, Apollodorus was angry. He said to Socrates, "What hurts me most is seeing you unjustly put to death."

Socrates answered, "Would you rather see me justly than unjustly put to death, my friend?"

Interpersonal problems in the church are something like that. It makes little difference if the issue is just or unjust, right or wrong. The heart of the problem is brothers and sisters in Christ are in conflict and pain. Our vocation demands we help them.

The Principle:
The Law of Mutual Benefit

The key to resolving interpersonal disputes is to look for a win/win solution. "I had to decide how to deal with the trustee chairman," recalls one pastor who did this. "He had expressed total opposition to fulfilling our church's financial obligation to the denomination. I had two choices: one, remove him from the board, or two, reorganize the board so he would not be involved in this decision. I chose number two, which led to a little conflict with him. In the long run, however, he saw the wisdom of what I did. He is now contributing to the church in his area of strength, and others are making the decisions for which he didn't show much talent."

To find the win/win situation demands creativity. Another pastor struggled with what to do with a Sunday school teacher with skewed doctrine: "His teaching was not entirely kosher. The class recognized that and asked me to stop him from teaching. I decided his slightly off-base teaching was the result of inexperience, not intentional error, and I thought he had good potential as a Bible teacher. I asked the class to stick with him while we paid for him to take a Bible correspondence course. Some class members left, but this teacher's skills grew by leaps and bounds, and most who left have returned."

Interpersonal disputes are solved neither by referring to an absolute standard of right and wrong nor by measuring the results against the effectiveness of the majority. When two people (or groups) are angry with one another in an interpersonal conflict, there is often no principle of right and wrong to follow. And just because some people have a larger family or following doesn't mean they should be given the benefit of the doubt.

The arbiter's role is to help the combatants see the value of making peace and then to discover a mutually beneficial resolution. This indeed is the nitty-gritty of church leadership. It's the apostle Paul pleading with Euodia and Syntyche to "agree with each other in the Lord" (Phil. 4:2).

Perhaps the best analogy is a parent trying to settle a dispute between two children over a toy. Neither child has any absolute right to the toy. It doesn't really make a difference to the parent (or even the children, in the long run) which one has it. But they have locked horns and are incapable of resolving the problem by themselves. The parent searches for the solution that will bring both a measure of happiness so the family can get on with things.

Some pastors have a knack for peacemaking. They intuitively sense others' feelings and the steps needed to negotiate a cease-fire. For the rest of us, it is helpful to keep in mind the major principle of interpersonal negotiations.

The Motivation:
The Law of Forgiveness

Counselors are aware of the importance of acceptance in dealing with counselees. Little progress is made until the counselee realizes the counselor accepts him or her as a person.

Similarly, little happens to heal the breach between two warring factions until each can accept the other, then truly forgive the offenders for real or perceived wrongs.

The pastor's role is not so much to dispense forgiveness in a priestly fashion as to create an atmosphere in which forgiveness can take place. To create a forgiving atmosphere, the pastor must be a forgiving person and have preached forgiveness regularly. Pastors are seen as agents of forgiveness. They are considered both forgivers themselves and persons qualified to promote forgiveness among others.

As catalysts of forgiveness, they need not fear compromising themselves or their church. Acts of forgiveness do not diminish the theological integrity of a church nor its institutional strength. Jesus said, "Blessed are the peacemakers, for they shall be called the children of God."[1] As we noted in our examination of Matthew 18 (see chapter 4), Jesus taught that the place to start with an angry disciple was not hard nosed application of law but a soothing dose of loving-kindness. The major roadblocks to forgiveness usually turn out to be ego and pride. As Chrysostom noted four hundred years after Christ, if you wish your wife to love you as the church loves Christ, "then take care of her as Christ did of the church. If you see her despising you, scorning you, and treating you with contempt, you can win her love by spending care on her. No bonds are more despotic than these."[2]

This is not a simple task. Forgiveness is foreign to human temperament, particularly to our modern temperament. We are taught to look out for number one, that turning the other cheek is foolish. In some sense modern society is like cultures where the concept of forgiveness doesn't exist. Working among the Chin tribe of Burma, early missionary linguists found the concept of forgiveness untranslatable into the language. When the missionaries explained the biblical concept and asked what word would correspond, the Chin replied, "We *never* do that to one who wrongs us." The missionaries eventually settled for a word that means "come face to face with" and then had to build on that concept the idea of truly forgiving a wrong.[3]

But just because the concept is foreign to our ears does not mean it cannot be accomplished. Pastors who intervene effectively can help bring about true forgiveness. David Seamands in his book *Healing for Damaged Emotions* offers five tests for forgiveness: First, can you thank God for the lessons learned in pain? Second, can you talk about the event without anger or feelings of revenge? Third, have you accepted your part of the blame for what happened? Fourth, can you revisit the scene without a negative reaction? Fifth, can you reward those who hurt you?[4]

These five tests represent the pastor's goal when intervening in interpersonal difficulties in the church. The goal is well worth the risk.

Dangers

Confusing the interpersonal with the theological. It is easy to confuse an interpersonal dispute with a theological one. We sometimes hope to find theology in an interpersonal conflict, because it's far easier to apply "law" than to reach a solution of mutual benefit. Law is clean and precise. Law does not demand the sticky problems of emotional involvement. Too rigid an application of the ethical may develop a few saints, but it leaves far more broken Christians along the way. Superimposing a theological answer on a problem that is at heart interpersonal may achieve a temporary truce, but the emotional rebellion will continue underground and eventually erupt in full-scale war.

For errors of doctrine, two steps are required:

1. Identify the error and point out the negative consequences;

2. Bring about reconciliation with God through the propositional application of Scripture.

For personal offenses, however, a three-step process is called for:

1. Identify the hurt and acknowledge the pain;

2. Forgive the offending party;

3. Bring about reconciliation through a face-to-face meeting between the two offended parties.

At times, people stop at step 2, saying they "forgive" the other person but not attempting true reconciliation. But an equal temptation for pastors is to bypass the second step, forgiveness, in the pell-mell race to reconciliation. Many a pastor, following the theological model, has brought together two warring factions before the groundwork of forgiveness was laid. The result is usually an emotional explosion.[5]

Confusing the interpersonal with the institutional. It is easier to say "This problem is a threat to our institution!" than to deal with the dynamics of interpersonal conflict. The first is the role of the professional manager, the second the role of the wounded healer.

One survey respondent began an anecdote by saying, "The pastor's job is doing what's best for the church." As a partial job description, that's correct; as the sum total, it falls far short. The pastor's job is manifold: teaching the gospel, doing what is best for the church, doing what is best for the individuals within the church, etc. If the second part is confused with the third, the result is a business/management outlook that rarely solves interpersonal problems.

It's not unusual for an interpersonal issue to be confused with an institutional one. Say a board chairman proposes a new program at a board meeting. Another member may strongly object, not so much because he doesn't like the idea, but because he's upset the chairman didn't consult him. The conflict is interpersonal — a perceived snub by the chairman — but the chairman doesn't realize it because the personal grievance is masked by concern for the institution: "But we've never done it that way before." This clinging to church tradition may or may not be what's best for the church, but no amount of clear-headed reasoning by the chairman will remove the objection. Interpersonal reconciliation is what's needed. If the board member objects to the chairman's ideas often enough, the chairman would be wise to first forgive him, and then sit down with him and explore what personal hurts may be driving the constant objections.

Confusing the interpersonal with the personal. It's tempting to take on the emotional burden of church members' arguments. That's understandable; generally pastors are caring people, sensitive to hurts in others. The danger arises when pastors make others' hurts their own; they sacrifice themselves (and unfortunately sometimes their families) to situations where they are supposed to be healers, not co-patients.

One pastor was counseling a woman whose husband constantly criticized her. He wanted the husband to come to a session so they could work through the issue, but he realized that deep down he just wanted to chew out the husband for being so cold and unfeeling. He had always liked the woman and found her attractive, so he had assumed her hurts. The pastor wisely waited several weeks before scheduling the session — until he could approach the situation more objectively.

An oxymoron, "caring objectivity," is called for to adequately deal with interpersonal conflict in the congregation.

Conclusion

J. I. Packer, in his classic work *Knowing God*, summed up the attitude of the pastor dealing with interpersonal risk: "You are called to be a meek man not always standing up for your rights nor concerned to get your own back or troubled in your heart by ill treatment and personal slights. (Though if you are normally sensitive, these things are bound to hurt you at the top level of consciousness.) You are simply to commit your cause to God and leave it to Him to vindicate you if and when He sees fit. Your attitude toward your fellow men, good and bad, nice and nasty, Christian and unbeliever, is to be that of the good Samaritan toward the Jew in the gutter: Your eyes must be open to see others' needs, both spiritual and material; your heart must be ready to care for needy souls when you find them; your mind must be alert to plan out the best way to help them; and your will must be set against the trick that we are all so good at — passing the buck, going by on the other side, and contracting out of situations of need where sacrificial help is called for."[6]

I don't believe I've read a better description of what can happen when that attitude is brought to situations involving people at odds in the church than this account from Jamie Buckingham's book *Coping with Criticism*:

"Several years ago I led an interdenominational conference for missionaries in Thailand. It was the first time the various Protestant and evangelical missionaries had ever come together with Roman Catholic priests and nuns for a teaching retreat. The first day was tense as some of the evangelicals were forced to interface with the Roman Catholics. However, by the end of the second day the atmosphere had cleared and it seemed the groups were actually going to be able to flow together in unity.

"The final afternoon, meeting in a large screened pavilion overlooking the gulf, I spoke on forgiveness. At the close of my teaching session, even before I had left the speaker's stand, a Roman Catholic nun stepped forward from the group. She was French and had been a missionary to the Thai people for a number of years. She knelt before me and crossed herself.

" 'For many years I have held deep grudges against the Protestants who came in to Thailand and built on the foundations built by the Catholic Church. I have been highly critical, and I need forgiveness. Will you pray for me?' I started to respond, for it was the very subject I had been teaching about. But as I stepped forward to pray for her, I felt checked. I stepped back and heard myself saying, 'No, sister, I am not the one to pray for you. You have made your confession and now you are absolved from your sin. I want to ask those here who have felt resentment or bitterness toward you to come and pray for you. In so doing, they will receive forgiveness themselves.'

"I stepped to one side and left her kneeling on the concrete floor of the screened pavilion where we were meeting. At once several people got to their feet and came forward. Then several others. In all there were almost a dozen men and women who stood around the kneeling nun. It was a touching moment. There were very few dry eyes in the room."[7]

Forgiveness does indeed solve interpersonal problems. It only takes people willing to risk themselves, their feelings, and their time in order to see that it happens.

PERSONAL RISKS

He that loses by getting, had better lose than get.

WILLIAM PENN

One of the hardest categories of risk to define is personal risk. Since any significant decision has an element of personal interest, to single out some risks and call them *personal* is somewhat artificial.

There is, however, a nexus of risks whose *primary* cause and motivation is the leader's personal interest. The most common of these deal with the ministerial career.

When a pastor moves from a successful pastorate to another church, the risk revolves around the fear of failure. A pastor who assumes a pastorate vacated by a preaching legend faces the prospect of failure in comparison with the predecessor. The pastor must weigh the risks of staying in the present church (stagnation or decline) versus the risks of going to the new one (failure by comparison).

Sometimes these crises are brought on by life-stage dynamics. British sociologist Elliot Jaques once examined the relationship between creativity and midlife in the lives of 310 painters, composers, writers, and other artists. He found a common crisis in the midthirties. For some — Dylan Thomas, Sinclair Lewis — it was a crisis of confidence from which they never recovered. For others — Beethoven, Goethe, Ibsen —

it spurred risk taking that led to great creative breakthroughs.[1]

Daniel Levinson and his fellow researchers at Yale found the patterns of life a person sets in his thirties, when he is concentrating on "making it," cannot last if he is to remain fulfilled afterwards. He must enlarge his circle, expand his interests, and seek new adventure, or he will wither on the vine.[2]

For pastors this may mean discovering God's new challenge for ministry. Churches' needs sometimes outgrow pastors' ministerial gifts. Perhaps in its early years the church needs a planter, organizer, and personal evangelist. As the church matures, the discipler, nurturing the congregation, becomes the church's crying need. Sometimes that calls for new leadership — and a difficult decision for pastor and board alike.

Or, sometimes pastors outgrow churches. New interests and skills lead the pastor to a larger responsibility, or the present church becomes routine, known, mastered, and the pastor needs a tough inner-city ministry to rescue or a new church to plant.

Other personal risks involve the pastor's family. One associate pastor told about a crisis he faced when his arthritic wife became dependent upon prescription drugs and her personality changed. She became extremely critical of the senior pastor and his children. She was suspicious of the people in the church, almost to the point of paranoia. At the same time, their teenage son became an alcoholic. Under the weight of such family concerns, he felt compelled to resign and start over elsewhere. The risk of change is sometimes forced on you; other times you are left to make the hard decision yourself.

Or the risk may involve personal dimensions within the present church — a reluctance to replace an old friend who hasn't attended a deacon meeting for a year, or turn down a family friend who wants to lead a Bible study but has no skills to do so. In most of these cases, the risks are simply theological, institutional, or interpersonal. But the minute a pastor's close friend is the subject of the decision, the personal element threatens to dominate the decision. Danger lies in confusing a personal decision with an institutional or theological one; that makes identification of a personal decision extremely important. Several questions help:

1. Choose someone in the church for whom you have *only* pastoral regard. Then ask: If this person were the subject of the decision instead of my good friend, would I decide as I'm tempted to now?

2. Am I deciding this way simply because I've been attacked or criticized by the people involved? If this had taken place before the criticism occurred, how would I have decided then?

3. Am I making this decision simply because I know I can handle this person in a special way? That is, is there some trait in this person, rather than the facts of the case, that is determining the way I handle the issue?

4. Am I making this decision simply because of the power I hold as leader? Wielding power is perhaps the most insidious of personal considerations, because how power is used depends on the "theology" one holds of the pastoral role. If your theology of the pastoral role calls for a strong, authoritarian leader, then all decisions are in a sense more personal than if you view the pastor as first among equals.

The Principle:
The Law of the Hippocratic Oath

Personal risks are guided by a principle followed by physicians: Heal, but in healing do no harm. A pastor taking a personal risk should be concerned, first and last, with doing no harm to the body of Christ or anyone in it.

King David writes in Psalm 69 of finding himself in deep trouble. He says he is "sinking in the miry depths where there is no foothold." His enemies are without number; they "seek to destroy" him — for no good reason. Yet David's concern is to not let his reaction to this unfair persecution adversely

75879

affect the body of Christ. "May those who hope in you not be disgraced because of me. O Lord, the Lord Almighty, may those who seek you not be put to shame because of me" (v. 6).

In personal decisions, whether to change churches or decide for or against a friend, the church leader must first of all "do no harm" to the ministry. The leader must constantly think, *The body of Christ has a higher priority than my career; I cannot make decisions that will harm the ministry.* If changes must be made, our survey showed, it is wise to make them slowly, surely, with preparation, restraint, and prayer — even when the circumstances have been unfair or you have been foully treated.

In most cases hurt and fault run on both sides. One pastor wrote: "My first pastorate lasted only six months. I had my head in the clouds with notions that this small church wanted me to lead them to the Promised Land. Several problems converged at once. People didn't feel I was preaching strongly enough against speaking in tongues. Many longed for the former pastor and worked against me to try to get him to return.

"I didn't handle that as maturely as I might have. I developed a judgmental attitude toward the status quo mentality of the church people. I was young and still dressed as a college student rather than a small-town pastor. I wore shirts and blue jeans downtown and made no pretense of acting 'like a preacher.' I didn't attempt to communicate on the level of the church people.

"I realized the level of animosity toward me was high enough and irrational enough that to have prolonged the ministry would have been counterproductive. I simply got off to a bad start, and there was no chance for things to be remedied. A quick departure was most merciful to all."

Such a departure, the most personal of all pastoral decisions, needs to be made with grace and with as much love as possible. The strength of the body of Christ is the bottom line for us all.

The Motivation:
Humility

The attitude we bring to personal decisions is not primarily obedience, nor is it commitment, or even forgiveness — though all of those certainly are personal virtues. The essential attitude to bring to personal decisions is humility.

Jonathan Edwards, in his classic *Religious Affections*, says: "Humility is the most essential thing in true religion . . . the great Christian duty is self-denial. This duty consists of two things: first, in denying worldly inclinations and its enjoyments and second, in denying self-exaltation and renouncing one's self-significance by being empty of self. . . . The humble Christian is more apt to find fault with his own pride than with that of other men. . . . A truly humble person who has a low view of his own righteousness and holiness is poor in spirit and modest in speech. . . . He is apt to put the best construction on others' words and behavior and to think that none is as proud as he is. But the proud hypocrite is picked to discern the mote in his brother's eye. He never sees the beam in his own. He's often crying out about someone else's pride, finding fault with that person's appearance and way of living. Yet he never sees the filthiness of his own heart."[3]

In the spring of 1986, I was part of a fact-finding trip to South Africa. We interviewed church leaders in that troubled country to find out what the church was doing in the face of cultural upheaval. One leader we interviewed was David Bosch, dean of the faculty of the University of South Africa. An accomplished teacher, researcher, and administrator, David was born and raised in South Africa. His Afrikaner nationality made him a part of the ruling minority. His efforts to renounce apartheid made him a hero to some factions and an enemy to others.

His accomplishments at the university gave him an opportunity to escape the turmoil and trouble: Princeton University in the United States offered him a tenured teaching position.

"After years of struggle, it was a chance to get away from it all. My children were grown. My wife was willing to go. Princeton is a great university. Yet over the interview process and the months of decision, the Lord made it clear he still had plans for us in South Africa. Finally, the command was so clear we could do nothing else. We turned down the offer at Princeton and will continue to work for the kingdom here in South Africa."

That's the spirit that must pervade any decision making that involves a leader's personal interest. Without it, mistakes will surely be made.

Dangers

The danger of making personal decisions by imposing theological constructs on them (that is, using the law of right and wrong) is what we might call *prophetism*. Personal preferences become holy absolutes. By marshaling Scripture to support a personal agenda, church leaders quickly go awry. New messiah is a long way from servant/leader.

Prophetism easily becomes neurotic. Generally, these leaders see their personal spiritual journey as the model for all spiritual journeys. Forgotten are "past" personality flaws and aberrant activities. Personal desire is labeled as God's revelation.

It is equally tempting to mix the institutional with the personal. Commitment to the church is noble. Sometimes, however, personal ambition gets mixed in, endangering the leader's spiritual well-being and the well-being of the leader's family. Dedication to God's work is thought to excuse overwork and neglect of health and family. Although workers in many professions suffer from this temptation, it has a particularly pernicious form in "call" situations, because the worker uses "God's call and mission" as the false rationale for workaholism. Most prospective workers in the mission field, for example, are bombarded with the overwhelming "needs" of the mission: "We *must* have replacements for retiring missionaries to keep the work going in such-and-such a country." The dynamic is hard to resist, whether overseas or in a local parish. The needs *are* overwhelming, and the job tantalizingly open-ended.

It is easy to confuse an interpersonal decision with a personal one. We are so influenced by our relationships and loved ones, it is difficult to get in touch with *our* needs in the matter. (Or more precisely, to get in touch with what God wants us to do in the matter.)

The dangers of treating a personal decision or risk as an interpersonal one are many. Self-righteousness is one. We can rationalize our decision as being essential to the welfare of a group of people. If true, this is an institutional concern. But usually leaders overestimate rather than underestimate the value of their presence.

Knowing when to leave is difficult. There are times to stay and fight through conflicts and down times, even if the eventual resolution is in doubt.

At times, though, staying can be more destructive than leaving. One pastor wrote the following story of mishandling such a situation: "A group of dissident members collaborated with some staff members to try to have me removed. They mailed a letter to members outlining their concerns. It included their names. After holding open meetings and trying to bring reconciliation, I finally led the church board to remove from the church role those who had signed the letter. We gave them the opportunity to change their minds and stop trying to remove me and be restored. However, over two hundred people — nearly half the congregation — left." In this instance, the cost of staying was probably too great and should not have been paid. At some point, one's personal ministry must be subordinated to the work of the body itself. The only way to solve a personal risk-taking situation is to approach it with humility, which is to approach it with a great deal of trembling, fear, and prayer for personal guidance.

Conclusion

A right decision triggers a sense of security, a certain peace of mind that comes from doing God's will. Marguerite Wolf, in an article, "The Meaning of Security," put it this way: "True security isn't a commodity to be bought or won in the future. It's a present state of mind. A satisfaction in being who you are and where you are, alone or in company."[4]

Making the right decision in a difficult personal situation leads to contentment and peace — contentment knowing it was done with the good of everyone in mind, and peace in knowing God has led and directed throughout.

I talked to a pastor last year, a friend who, after a series of good early pastorates, had spent the last ten years in a large, well-to-do church in a Kansas City suburb. But now, at fifty-two years of age, he sensed his effectiveness there had peaked. His question to me was, "Should I hang on here for another ten years until I can retire? Or should I look for another place to serve?

I asked, "Do you have another church in you? Do you want to climb one more mountain?"

After a moment's reflection, he said, "Yes, I think I do. Thanks for putting the question in that way. I think I can serve God more effectively in a new church that is still on the way up."

He resigned his secure position and after some searching found a church of two hundred in another midwestern community where he has recently begun his pastorate.

God gives us personal challenges of many different kinds during our ministries. Our task is to listen and respond — with humility.

NINE

WHEN CATEGORIES AREN'T CLEAR

It is only by risking our persons from one hour to another that we live at all. And often enough our faith beforehand in an uncertified result is the only thing that makes the result come true.

WILLIAM JAMES

As you probably have sus-
pected, there isn't always a clear-cut distinction between theological, institutional, interpersonal, and personal decisions.
Many risks combine elements from several categories. One
pastor remembered a particularly difficult example.

"We had a highly gifted young man in our church. He was
well-loved, a graduate student, our youth group sponsor. He
seemed to everyone a devoted, responsible person. He and
his wife were especially close to another couple in the church
with several children. John became close to one of them, an
elementary school boy — so close that during a period of
severe academic and marital stress, John became involved in
some sexual games with this youngster.

"I'd had a particularly exhausting week. The church had
been through several tragedies in the past month. People
were torn up, and I preached that morning as best I could
from depleted reserves. Then I had a funeral service *after*
evening service — I didn't get home until a quarter to eleven.
Thinking I had finally coped with all the problems, I tried to
relax.

"At 11:15 the phone rang. It was a church leader calling to

tell me his son had been molested by their good friend and our youth leader, John. They had filed a complaint with the police but wanted me to know. That way if I wanted to help prepare John and his wife (she knew nothing about it yet) I could.

"I knew I had to act immediately. If a policeman knocked at the door, John's wife would be devastated. I called John and told him I had to see him and his wife immediately at the church. I called the elders and asked them to meet us there. When I arrived seven people were already waiting.

"I knew there would be hostility and confusion. From 11:30 until 2:30 that morning, we talked through the whole thing. When John realized it wasn't a lynching party, he relaxed somewhat. He confessed and was very remorseful. We tried to balance kindness and truth with confrontation and concern. You can imagine the gut-wrenching experience it was.

"Until then, I'd had a great pastoral relationship with both families. Now I was caught in the middle. Based on past experiences, everyone should have trusted me. Given the circumstances, I felt that no one did.

"As elders, we had to deal with the spiritual side of the question with John, but we also had to be concerned with the well-being of the body. Were other children involved? John said no. I believed him (and it turned out there never were). But at the time, all the kids he had contact with were potential victims. What to do about them and their families?

"Timing was a problem. We decided that to go public with the news before properly dealing with John and his wife would be counterproductive. So we waited until legal authorities acted before we made any public statement. This was not a popular decision. Mothers of other boys were incensed later that we had not immediately gone public with the story. I had spent the evening with one family the day before the news broke. They were extremely upset that I hadn't said anything to them about it.

"After it was over, we still had to figure out what to do as a church about the legal obligations. Some were forgiving while others remained extremely bitter.

"Up to this point, I thought we had handled the pastoral aspects well, both with John and the church as a whole. I'm not sure we did as well with the legal aspects. Because I had heard John's confession that Sunday night in front of others, I had to testify when subpoenaed. John's family held that against me. They felt I had taken advantage of John. They said he had understood what he said to me wouldn't be held against him in court. None of us were thinking about that at the time. We were acting as a church, not as arresting officers.

"I didn't testify willingly. I pleaded with the grand jury not to subpoena me — they could have subpoenaed others — but they subpoenaed me. One question was, 'In your opinion, was his confession in the priestly relationship?' I said, 'No, other people were present.' Further, according to state law, anyone, including clergy, who receives information of child molestation is obligated to report it.

"I did more — and as I look back, it may have been too much. In my concern for John, I checked out legal options for him and recommended an attorney. Eventually John was sent to prison. Unfortunately, the attorney turned out to be a hotshot, and because I had been candid about my role in trying to mediate the situation with all parties, the attorney tried to talk John's family into suing me for violation of confidentiality.

"As a result of this experience, I would counsel pastors to be cautious when dealing with attorneys. Openness can get you into trouble. I simply didn't understand some of the implications of the questions they asked. Frankly, you need your own attorney.

"I also talked with the district attorney; after the judgment, I tried to do some plea bargaining. I felt I went more than the second mile, yet looking back, I wonder if some of my efforts were counterproductive.

"There are no simple steps to take in this situation. Usually when something bad happens, you can look back and say, 'This, this, and this were probably mistakes. And this is what I did right.' But in this case, I still wonder how I could have ministered to everyone any differently. The concerns were so diverse and in many cases conflicting.

"My ministry had been productive at that church. I had been there four years and planned to stay a long time. But after this, my effectiveness was greatly reduced. I came to realize there are times in ministry when you have to make decisions that may destroy your long-term effectiveness with some people. It's the nature of the job. Some transitions are part of the game.

"God used me at that church, then moved me to a new situation. I came through a tough situation, and now God is using me in a different context."

Analysis

This case involves all of the four categories: theological (pastoral concern for John's spiritual well-being), institutional (the church's relationship with the community and its legal requirements), interpersonal (ministry to the families of the other boys in the church), and when we consider the impact the events had on the pastor's family and career, it also has elements of a personal risk. How does a leader attack such a complex problem?

First, recognize one methodology alone won't work. It is useless to reduce the whole thing to a theological question, say, and deal with it on the basis of the Law of Right and Wrong. That approach will satisfy certain portions of the problem but will only exacerbate others.

Second, break the situation into its components. Usually thinking through the people involved helps to demarcate the types of risks. Dealing with John is one part of the problem. Dealing with the elders is another, while dealing with the police and lawyers is a third. A fourth would be dealing with the mothers of other children. Each of these components requires a different risk-taking style.

In this case, the pastor instinctively tried to do this, with some success. With John, the pastor showed compassion and forgiveness. He acted out of concern for his spiritual and emotional well-being. He did his best to cushion the blow for John's wife and spent time assuring them of the church's support, all the while never losing sight of the seriousness of the problem and the need for upholding the theological requirement for confession of sin. The pastor managed to treat John's sin as something to be put away and overcome, all the while telling John himself of the possibility of forgiveness and the surety of the church's love.

With the elders the pastor walked a similar tightrope, balancing the need to uphold the theological integrity of the church with the need to put the institution in a position to comply with state law. He did not succumb to the temptation to overplay the theological by denying the existence or value of the law of the land, nor did he ignore the theological implications of the situation simply to satisfy law enforcement officials.

As he admits, he probably erred most in dealing with the lawyers — trying to deal with them on an interpersonal level rather than with institutional principles. As a result, they tried to take advantage of his candor.

He also admits failing to satisfy the mothers of other children in the church. But this he explains (accurately, I think) not as a result of his failure but as the result of being forced onto the horns of a dilemma that could not be resolved to the satisfaction of all.

Third, recognize that some problems have no satisfactory answers. Some situations offer no good solutions, only choices between bad and worse. For some reason, in this fallen world God sometimes uses suffering and evil as his schoolroom to teach humility and grace. We must be prepared, in the face of impossible problems that we know will eventually lead to a change of churches, to submit to God's unknown purposes. Faith becomes most meaningful when we are faced with the meaninglessness of tragedy, sin, and suffering.

TEN

HOW IMPORTANT IS IT?

There are two sorts of risk in every opportunity: uncertainty about feasibility and uncertainty about the benefits.

Edward de Bono

Identifying the nature of the issue involved, whether theological, institutional, interpersonal, or personal, is the essential first step. But once we ask what kind of risk we're facing, a second major question needs to be asked: *How important is it that we make this decision?*

Take, for instance, the case of one pastor in the Southeast:

"Our district superintendent put me in charge of a regional camp for six churches. He wanted to start a summer youth conference, and his plan was to have a one-week camp. I checked facilities and talked to the pastors to find out how many of their people would be interested. My research showed two things: the cost was too high and the anticipated participation too small to support a week-long camp. I reported this to the superintendent, and we decided to change to an overnight retreat.

"Then I found out the district had never held an overnight camp before. Further, the district had never been well organized, and there was little sense of community among these churches.

"I told the district superintendent, 'I don't think the people are going to accept this idea, at least not this first year.'

"He wasn't so sure. He asked me to come to the district board meeting and present my information: prices, locations, and my impressions. I did and suggested an alternative for the first year: an all-day picnic. 'We won't have to rent a facility, the people won't have to stay overnight, and it won't be such a drastic innovation,' I said. 'It would be something we can handle financially no matter what happens, and we'll be building for an overnight camp in years to come.'

"The superintendent said, 'I'd really like to go with an overnight activity.' He pushed. 'You don't feel good about that, do you?'

"I said, 'No, I don't. I don't want to cop out by having only a picnic, but I think it's the only thing that will work.' He persisted, however, and finally I gave in. He gave me $45 to put down on a facility and told me to do the best I could.

"I still didn't feel good about it, but I didn't feel the issue was important enough to object more than I did."

The ambiguity in such decisions rests in the fact that taking a risk in any situation is essentially a two-step process. The "scientific" core of a decision is the determination of how risky the situation is. At this fact-gathering stage, the pastor acts as an objective observer, reading people's emotional states, factoring in probable consequences, thinking of alternatives.

However, even after the facts are in, the decision still needs to be made — usually on the basis of a value commitment (the second stage). In this pastor's case, he placed the value of good relationships with his district superintendent above having to prove his analysis correct.

In making these decisions, the pastor is acting like any good administrator. Consider the question of the use of the insecticide DDT. William Lowrance in his book *Of Acceptable Risk* traces the history of this important insecticide that won chemist Paul Müller the Nobel Prize in 1948.

After World War II a general insecticide was urgently needed. The spread of typhus by body lice, malaria by mosquitoes, and typhoid and dysentery by flies threatened health worldwide.

As early as March, 1945, the Department of Agriculture and the Department of the Interior recognized DDT could be harmful to fruits and vegetables (and thus eventually human beings), but initially DDT's perceived benefits exceeded its dangers. However, continued studies added to the pressure to discontinue its use. In 1972 the Environmental Protection Agency (EPA) banned the use of DDT.

The decision was a difficult one. The EPA based its decision on a 577-page report that itself presented mixed views. Its conclusion: "With the evidence now in, DDT can be regarded neither as a proven danger as a carcinogen for man nor as an assuredly safe pesticide; suspicion has been aroused and it should be confirmed or dispelled."

The statistics did not conclusively decide the issue. The final decision was based not on the numbers but on other values of our society. As in many church decisions, values conflicted. We need effective pesticides to maintain high agricultural productivity. We also need to protect society from the long-term residues of such pesticides. When the EPA discontinued the use of DDT, food prices skyrocketed. Famines worsened; malaria and other diseases controlled by DDT increased dramatically in several parts of the world. The case richly illustrates the difficulties of risk-taking situations.[1]

Measurement

Step one in measuring a decision's importance is to develop a measuring tool. Chapter 13 introduces such a tool for church leaders. After surveying one thousand local church leaders about tough decisions they have made, we ranked the relative risk of their most frequent decisions. Using this data, we put together a scale to measure a decision's relative risk.

Obviously such data does not by itself decide an issue. Before a patient enters surgery, the physician informs him or her of the risk, usually with a hair-raising list of possible negative consequences: brain damage, paralysis, etc. A few patients decide to delay the surgery, or avoid it altogether, if it's an elective procedure. Most choose to go ahead, however, in spite of the risk. The statistics did not determine their choice, but they informed it.

Similarly, knowing how risky a decision is can prepare a church leader to make that decision.

Values

In some situations, values override risk statistics. Some religious truths, for example, we should be willing to risk everything for — even life itself. There are points of principle (although probably not as many as we think) for which we should be willing to risk our position of leadership. Even in those cases, however, knowing the numbers can help one strategize the approach to the decision. Greater care needs to be taken in high-risk cases.

Other issues are not so obvious in importance. One pastor remembers an incident where conflicting values (in this case efficiency versus institutional harmony) clouded his decision:

"A lady who had served as secretary of the church board for several years was unable to type, gossiped about board discussions in the community, and had a severely negative attitude. I wanted to remove her as secretary, which sounds like an easy decision until you realize she was related to the dominant family in the church, which represented three-fourths of the leadership and about one-third of the membership. What should I do — keep people happy or increase office efficiency?"

Another factor making value judgments difficult is the pastor's feelings. Church leaders must withstand a certain amount of pressure and attack without letting it affect judgment-making ability. One pastor remembered: "One woman, during a church softball game, lost her temper and treated me in a disrespectful way. The hardest part for me was to finally decide to do what the Scriptures plainly say in Matthew 18:15: confront her. This woman is more outspoken than anyone else in the church; her husband was chairman of the board of trustees. Everyone in the congregation looks to her for leadership. But I felt I had to confront her."

Deciding the importance of an issue can be a lonely, subjective job. Enlisting the help of others in the church is essential, particularly the assistance of the leaders. They articulate the mission of the church. They hire (or ratify the hiring of) the pastor, and the pastor needs to match his or her ranking of values with theirs.

Group decisions, however, tend to be more risk oriented than individual decisions, particularly when the ruling group is relatively homogeneous. Sociological studies have shown that when birds of a feather flock together, they push one another toward more extreme decisions. It's as if they give one another the courage to move further than may be wise.

Sociologists call this phenomenon the "risky shift."[2] The more homogeneous the group, the more likely it is to shift toward risky decisions. The church leader needs to consider the board a valuable resource to avoid personal subjectivity, but at some point he or she needs to correct for the danger of "committee only" decisions. The individual does boast some advantages over the group in decision making.

Ernest Beevers, pastor of West Hills Baptist Church in Coraopolis, Pennsylvania, developed an analytical tool that has proved helpful (see Chart 5). He uses an X–Y grid on which the X-coordinate represents degree of certainty, answering the question, "How sure am I that I am right?" The Y-coordinate represents the degree of importance, or "How important is this matter to me?" Each coordinate moves from one to five, five representing the issues about which a leader feels most strongly.

Beevers uses the example of handling the toothpaste tube: "I'm absolutely certain the tube should be rolled from the bottom, so on the X-coordinate I give a five. However, I don't think it is a very important issue, so on the Y-coordinate I give a one. I will not break fellowship with my wife if she persists in squeezing the toothpaste tube in the middle. I've even decided not to rant and rave about the matter."

As an opposite example, Beevers cites the matter of

CHART 5

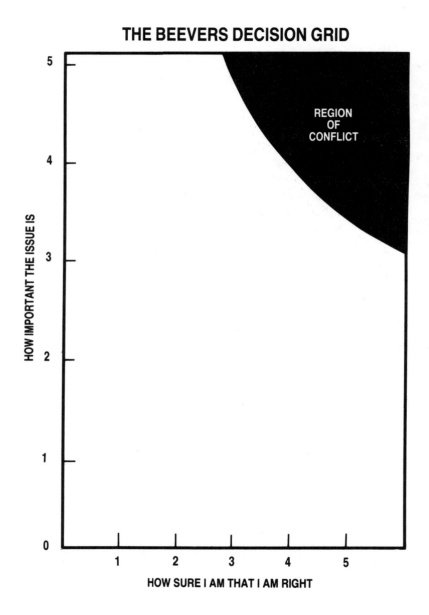

THE BEEVERS DECISION GRID

REGION
OF
CONFLICT

HOW IMPORTANT THE ISSUE IS

HOW SURE I AM THAT I AM RIGHT

whether to prolong life by artificial means. The importance of the issue is a definite five on the Y-scale. However, there is quite a difference of opinion on the question so the degree of certainty is less than five.

Any decision that falls in the shaded portion of the chart is an action issue. We are usually willing to go to the wall for issues in that area. Other quadrants indicate cautious action or none at all.

Another way to determine the relative importance of an issue is to answer a set of questions regarding it. Although pastors will develop their own set, the following list gives a feel for the process:

— Is this risk necessary?
— Can I reach my goal any other way?
— Is the potential loss greater than the potential gain?
— What can I lose by taking this risk?
— How will I know I'm losing?
— What can I do to prevent these losses from occurring?
— What do I need to know before taking this risk?
— Why don't I know it already?
— Who else can tell me what I need to know?
— Who else should know about the risk? Why?

Once a pastor knows the importance of an issue to himself, the church, and the other people involved, he can begin to determine more specifically whether the risk must be taken.

ELEVEN

WHAT ARE THE CIRCUMSTANCES?

Time makes more converts than reason.

THOMAS PAINE

An automobile operates by a series of explosions. Gasoline is mixed with air and ignited. Were these explosions to take place in an open area, they would destroy the engine. They take place, however, inside a piston chamber surrounded by steel walls. The walls protect the engine from negative effects of the explosions and, in fact, turn them into a force that drives the piston and makes automobiles remarkably efficient vehicles of travel.

Risks in ministry, like these explosions, can be very destructive if allowed to take place in an uncontrolled way. With proper safeguards, however, these explosions can propel the church forward. The question, of course, is how do we build safety chambers strong enough to withstand the explosions?

The Leader's Credibility

The first factor to consider is your stage in ministry. The axiom proves true: Don't make major changes in the first two years of ministry; establish trust first.

Our survey asked pastors to describe situations where they had to leave a church under pressure. A follow-up question asked what they might have done differently to forestall the firing. The most frequent response by far was typified by one pastor: "It was my first church. I did a lot of stupid things and made so many mistakes it's hard to see what I could have done differently."

Studies of graduating seminarians show the first year of ministry is one of the most dangerous times for a pastor. Many leave the ministry for good because of a crisis situation during that time. It is difficult to recover from mistakes of inexperience.

Our research indicated an equally dangerous time later in ministry, in the forty- to fifty-year age bracket. It appears that pastors are at risk during a "ministerial midlife crisis."

In an article in the *Presbyterian Survey*, pastor Eugene Timmons outlined a "six-stage cycle" most ministers go through. His observations put handles on the different kinds of conflict a pastor can expect as the years pass in a church:

He calls the first stage the "honeymoon," a time when minor mistakes are overlooked as long as major embarrassments do not occur.

The second he calls the "shakedown." The shakedown begins when "lay people stop denying that they do not like some of the things about the pastor and his or her ministry." It's important for the pastor at this stage to work to hear the criticisms and try to deal objectively with them. He or she should take the criticisms as part of the continuing trust-building process.

The third stage Timmons labels "early conflict." In this stage the pastor may begin to pick up a few feelings of distrust or dislike. A list of people with hard feelings towards the pastor develops, whether written or not. At this stage, people confront the pastor more openly, whereas in previous stages they would either have swallowed their criticisms or expressed them covertly.

The fourth stage is when the leadership itself (the elder board, the deacons, or whatever) feels free to make a move. Sometimes they will openly confront the pastor, but more often the really disenchanted ones will decline to serve. New leaders, less experienced, will take their place, and the pastor finds himself in a training situation.

The fifth stage is the "righteous cause" stage, where the pastor feels secure and comfortable enough to take the initiative, rather than merely answer criticisms and adjust the ministry to suit the whims of the congregation.

In the sixth stage the new leadership sees problems itself and begins to talk like the old leadership.[1]

It's helpful for pastors contemplating risk-taking decisions to decide where they are in this cycle. The stage itself doesn't determine the decision. But it can help pastors identify the amount of influence and power they have available, and thus accurately gauge the work to be done to execute the decision successfully. Stages don't always have to be described in terms of conflict. The six stages above could be translated into the language of trust. How much trust have I developed in my years in this church? Who, and how many, in this congregation will help me with my ideas for more effective ministry?

Realizing that the answers to these questions vary from year to year helps a minister avoid being surprised by lack of support — or the abundance of it.

Shared Responsibility

The second safeguard is to bring people in on a decision to act as a buffer and support. If the decision doesn't directly threaten or frighten the board, it is the natural group to include. At any rate, the leaders somehow need to be involved in the decision. If they are sympathetic, they become allies in the risk-taking decision.

At times, however, a pastor needs to win grassroots support, even though not all leaders back the decision. One pastor faced such a situation:

"The board had talked over the budget, and we had made the changes we thought necessary. When the budget was presented to the church for ratification, one board member, who had been through the whole budgeting process and voted for our budget, stood and said, 'I don't see why we have so much money going to outreach. We've never had money for local outreach before. I think we should pay the pianist instead.'

"I thought to myself, *You're a former pastor! You have to know better.*

"I had to make a quick decision whether to say anything. I don't like getting into an argument in front of the church, but I couldn't stay silent. So I gave a few reasons for the outreach program. Then I said that paying the pianist was going inward instead of outward. This was the first time in our church's history that we'd had some extra money to put into outreach, and I thought it important to do it.

"I didn't know how the church would react. They had been through some hard times, and most had the idea it's best not to rock the boat. In this case, I had one key element going for me. The pianist this board member wanted to pay was his wife. Even people who didn't want to rock the boat could see the self-interest. His idea was voted down.

"Afterwards many people came to me and said, 'I don't think his idea was good. Thanks for taking a stand.' Only one person objected.

"In making that decision to speak out, I was weighing the good of the church against this man's personal agenda. I had done my homework with the board, but at times you have to risk an open battle to woo the power of the whole congregation."

Pastors are odd mixtures of Lone Rangers and coalition makers. In some cases they must operate as if no one else in the world can or will help. As a short-range strategy, most of us can operate this way. As a long-range strategy, however, the pastor must draw on the full resources of lay power.

The pastor is somewhat like a motorboat propeller. The propeller can run for a short time out of water. However, it is built to run against the resistance of water; when it runs without that, it keeps increasing in velocity until the engine burns out. Lone Ranger pastors do the same. Pastors are built to run in a sea of people. When they don't have that resistance, they spin themselves into burnout, or they send the church careening in odd directions. Either way, ministry eventually comes to a standstill.

Occasionally, pastors are put in the position of taking Lone Ranger actions because they function as spokespersons for the church's silent majority. The issue may be a sensitive one that no one else in the church wants to support publicly. Such situations greatly increase the risk of the decision.

Timing

Proper timing is one of the most crucial of safeguards. There are two extremes: *hastiness,* where circumstances have not sufficiently ripened for action to be taken; and *procrastination,* where the proper moment came and went, lost because of indecision, fear, or laziness. Between those two extremes waits the proper moment to take a risk, and the leader is constantly searching for that moment.

Jesus knew the value of proper timing. In the seventh chapter of John, Jesus refused his brothers' invitation to go to Jerusalem for the Feast of Tabernacles because "for me the right time is not yet come." Later, however, after his brothers had gone to the feast, Jesus went, arriving about halfway through. Either time was risky for Jesus to go to Jerusalem. The Pharisees and temple authorities were seeking to arrest him and have him killed. Jesus, however, chose to take the risk (a risk to his life by the Jewish authorities) at one time and not the other because for his purposes (to teach in the temple) it was wiser to delay the trip. Perhaps the increased crowds in the middle of the festival afforded him a better chance of being heard.

The key to good timing is knowing when the people involved are prepared for the decision. On our survey, the second most frequently mentioned ingredient of good decision making was taking the time to prepare key people. One pastor explained: "I tend to bring people along with me in my reasoning and decision-making process, so there aren't surprises. That means *I* rarely get surprised."

Here's a list of questions helpful in deciding the right timing:

What would be the perfect time to act? Will that time ever come?

What would be the worst time to act?

What makes the risk necessary now?

What would happen if, after making preparations, I didn't risk now?

Will it ever be any easier?

Have my preparations created any impact? Are the people who should be taking my preparations seriously doing so?

Can I turn back? When is the last time I can turn back? Will things be the same as before if I turn back? What will have changed?

What other preparations do I have to make?

Personal Preparation

The fourth safeguard is to acquaint oneself thoroughly with the problem and all foreseeable ramifications. The "content" of what you're about to do must be mastered. This is not a time for winging it.

The emotions of a risk-taking situation are so difficult that the factual elements of the case need to become second nature to the risk taker. A salesman so masters his product line and sales pitch that in making the actual presentation, he can concentrate solely on modifying the presentation as he gets feedback from his audience. Pastors do the same.

Adequate resources exist to aid pastors in this preparation. Management literature on decision making abounds; with some modification it can be most helpful in the local church setting. Simple research techniques, particularly from the social sciences, can teach a pastor how to collect and evaluate the data of a complex sociological setting. Colleagues in ministry usually will lend a sympathetic and evaluative ear to your problem.

Perhaps the most interesting statistic from our survey arose from the answers to our question about biblical models pastors had used in their decision-making process. Of the many biblical decision makers mentioned, Jesus and Paul were named most frequently. Interestingly, among the respondents who had at one time or another been fired, not one mentioned they used Jesus as a model. Among those who had never been fired, however, Jesus was the most frequently mentioned model. A number of factors in Jesus' decision making may explain the correlation, but certainly a key one was Jesus' relentless attention to personal preparation.

Considering the circumstances naturally leads to another question one needs to ask before taking a risk: *What can I handle?* The personal temperament of the risk taker provides the major factor not only in deciding if the risk should be taken but in developing the strategy for taking the risk. To that question we now turn.

TWELVE

WHAT CAN I HANDLE?

So far as we are human, what we do must be either evil or good; so far as we do evil or good, we are human; and it is better, in a paradoxical way, to do evil than to do nothing; at least we exist.

T. S. ELIOT

I. D. Thomas, in *A Word from the Wise,* tells the story of a Georgia farmer living in a dilapidated shack. He hadn't planted anything, so nothing needed to be cultivated. The farmer just sat, ragged and barefoot, surrounded by the evidence of his laziness.

A stranger stopped for a drink of water and asked, "How's your cotton doing?"

"Ain't got none," replied the farmer.

"Didn't you plant any?"

"Nope. 'fraid of boll weevils."

"Well," continued the visitor, "how's your corn?"

"Didn't plant none. 'fraid there wasn't gonna be no rain."

"How are your potatoes?"

"Ain't got none. Scared of potato bugs."

"Really? What did you plant?"

"Nothin'," was the reply. "I just played safe."[1]

The church leader who never takes risks quickly finds: No risks, no returns.

The Bible supplies many instances of this Law of Risklessness. Proverbs predicts the nonrewards the sluggard can expect. Jesus' parable of the talents rests on the futility of trying to avoid all risk.[2]

Similarly, our survey showed that the risks of not taking a risk are the riskiest of all. Leaders who made few or no major decisions per year, regardless of category, were the most likely to have been dismissed from a church at some time in their ministry (see Chart 6).

This doesn't mean risk taking is something one merely decides to do and does. Even those outgoing souls who thrive on the thrill of risk sometimes have to force themselves to act — and will readily admit to the need to continually sharpen their skills.

For some, though, risk taking seems next to impossible. They would sooner tame a lion than confront a parishioner. For them, it is not a question of wanting to take a risk; it is a question of going against the natural inclinations of their personalities to resist conflict at all costs.

Such resistance is not to be taken lightly — nor demeaned. The third-century Turks told a fable about a soft wax candle that was lamenting the fact that the slightest touch injured it. The candle felt cheated by this apparent personality flaw. How the candle admired the rock-hard bricks, impervious to dents and nicks. Seeing that bricks started out as soft clay and only grew hard from heat, the candle had an idea. To acquire the brick's hardness and durability, the candle leaped into the fire, melted, and was consumed. The moral? It is useless to malign the "disadvantages" inherent in our personalities.[3]

Psychologist Frank Farley has identified a cluster of characteristics that make up the "Type T personality," high-profile people who are risk takers and daring adventurers. The roster of Type T's includes such people as DNA researcher Sir Francis Crick and aviator Amelia Earhart. Type T's prefer uncertainty to certainty, complexity to simplicity, and novelty to familiarity. They prefer to work in flexible structures and tend to be stifled by the 9-to-5 mentality.

At the opposite end of the personality spectrum are Type t (little t) personalities, people who avoid risks. People at this end of the personality spectrum are rarely public figures. Farley thinks big T's and little t's are determined largely

CHART 6

NOT TAKING A RISK: THE CASUALTY RATE

The bars here compare the two groups of respondents, Fired and Not Fired, according to their reluctance to make three types of tough decisions in a year: theological, institutional, and interpersonal. In each category, our research showed that the Fired group was more reluctant than the Not Fired group to make a decision.

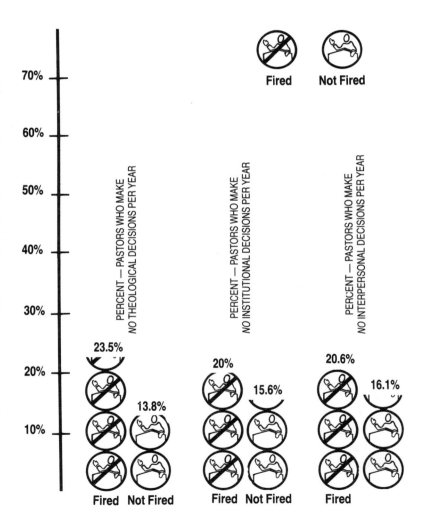

through genetics, though very early experiences may play a role.[4]

Little t's don't relish decisions, even when the groundwork has been laid and the time appears right. Witness a little-t pastor in action:

"Recently our board considered putting ceiling fans in the sanctuary. We talked about the advantages and the disadvantages. I was for the fans because they're economical. They blow the warm air back down in the winter; in the summer they create a breeze, so we don't have to run our air conditioner as often.

"Some on the board, however, didn't want to risk destroying the appearance of the sanctuary. We have a beautiful cathedral ceiling, and who knows for sure what hanging fans would do to the look.

"After all the discussion, we took a vote. The tally was five votes for the fans, three opposed. A split vote is unusual for our board, but the people who voted against the fans accepted it calmly, saying in effect, 'We voted against it, but that's the decision of the board and we'll support the decision. Let's get it done.'

"But I haven't purchased the fans. My head tells me they will save money — the facts support that. My head also tells me the fans will be accepted by the congregation. But my gut tells me not to do it, that it's not that necessary. I've thought about why I'm dragging my feet. If it had been an eight-to-nothing vote, I think I'd still feel uneasy. And I can't quite say why. Something is just telling me not to do it. It's a very real feeling, though not quantifiable.

"Actually, I'm causing more trouble for myself. Since the committee voted for the fans, I'm supposed to buy them. If I don't, I have to explain why I haven't and then get them to agree *not* to do it. But I just don't feel right about it."

This pastor simply does not have the temperament of a Nathan Hale, the Revolutionary War spy who, when about to be hanged, said he only regretted he had but one life to give for his country. Some church leaders (Hale himself probably would have been a minister had not the American Revolution broken out) have the bravado and gusto of a Hale. Others don't, and struggle with what to do.[5]

Although big T's take to risk taking more easily, little t's *can* develop confrontational skills. But they need to use the skills in ways congruent with their personalities. They are more likely to learn confrontational techniques through analytical descriptions — by the book, perhaps — than through actual experiences (which they may be too timid ever to initiate). People with little-t temperaments can be taught to take risks; it simply is more difficult for them.[6]

Even people with insecure personalities are risk takers of a sort, although they normally choose risks of a different category. Psychologist John Atkinson showed that two motivations drive people to take risks. One is the motivation to achieve; the other is the motivation to avoid failure. Those motivated to achieve generally take regular, consistent, intermediate risks. Those motivated to avoid failure go to one extreme or another. They either play it unusually safe, trying to avoid risk altogether, or they make extremely risky moves. The person who sinks his life savings in a speculative stock venture after a lifetime of passbook savings is typical of the avoid-failure personality.[7]

It's possible to analyze personality based on another polarity. The difference between the way intuitive personalities and rationalistic personalities take risks has been studied by Nathan Kogan and Michael Wallach. They found that intuitives tend to see the big picture better. They scan long-range implications of success or failure more quickly than others, and thus tend to take risks and force confrontations earlier. Those who have a more rationalistic orientation, on the other hand, tend to focus on the immediate and overlook the need for risk taking or confrontation until too late. Intuitively, Kogan and Wallach see the optimal personality to be a balance between the two.[8]

A third polarity has been drawn between the perfectionistic personality and the nonperfectionistic personality. Perfectionists are generally motivated by the fear of making mistakes. They are unusually cautious and averse to risk taking. Those with the nonperfectionistic personality, on the other hand, are more willing to put things up for grabs. David D. Burns, in his book *Feeling Good*, says, "Show me a man who can't stand to be wrong and I'll show you a man who's afraid to take risks and who has given up the capacity for growth. I probably make three mistakes in every therapy session."[9]

None of the personality experts who study risk taking discounts the possibility of people predisposed to not taking chances learning to do so. All would agree that training and experience have a great deal to do with a person's risk-taking skill. Those who trade futures on the Chicago Board of Trade, for example, learn to take risks; their living depends on it. Training for such a position involves gaining a good grasp of the statistical probabilities of various situations — and learning to analyze one's intuitions.

Few church leaders are trained in risk taking, although decision-making courses are becoming more common in seminaries. Still, they are far down the priority pole in divinity training. Most of us then, regardless of personality, develop risk-taking skills on the job. Here are some tactics to further our skills and help us determine what risks we can and cannot handle.

Tactics: Short-Range

First, take a reading of the emotional climate of the risk-taking situation. Focus particularly on your emotional situation by asking these questions:

Am I ever a little irrational? Is this one of those times? How do I know? What can I do about it?

Am I afraid? If yes, of what? If not, why not?

Am I ready to act? Will I ever be ready to act? What is holding me back?

It's equally productive to determine the emotional involvement you have in this particular project. Helpful questions to consider:

What feeling am I trying to express by taking this risk?

Will people think better or worse of me if I succeed? Do I care?

Do I care what opinion people have of me? What opinion of me would I like people to assume?

Second, convince yourself of the need to act. Sometimes action needs to be immediate. Make sure you consciously decide to act promptly or else have good, valid reasons for delay. Remember stories like the following:

"One of the elders, a pillar of the church who had been around seemingly forever, became angry over a church financial decision. The board decided to allocate some money to a project Bradley didn't like. It was obvious to everyone as he left the board meeting that he was very upset. I knew I needed to talk to him immediately, but I believed it was usually good policy to let things cool a little. In this case it wasn't. The next morning I had Bradley's resignation as an elder on my desk.

"I prayed over that letter, then next afternoon I went to his house. We spent the afternoon together, and by the end of the afternoon, although we still disagreed on the financial matter, he had withdrawn the resignation. We saw that in Christ we can have differences and still fellowship.

"I will be forever grateful to God for leading me to work it out quickly with Bradley. Over the next sixteen months, we became dear friends. We shared intimate times; he became a confidant for me.

"Bradley was a farmer. He had a small front-loading tractor, and one day he was carrying a load of stones in the front hopper. He went up a small grade — probably not more than two feet high — but it was enough to cause the load to shift, and it rolled that tractor over on top of him. He was killed instantly.

"I went out to the house. The medics had laid him under a blanket, still in the yard. His wife was in the kitchen. There was nothing I could do except put my arms around her and cry with her.

"Later I thought, *What if I hadn't talked with him when he wanted to resign?* I would have regretted it forever. As it is, I can rejoice in the friendship God gave us."

Tactics: Long-Range

Define your style. Ellen Siegelman in her book, *Personal Risk*, has developed an informal self-test that measures risk-taking style. She defines three categories: anxious risk takers, balanced risk takers, and careless risk takers. Knowing your style can help you prepare for a risk. For example, an anxious risk taker needs to push himself to make the decision. A careless risk taker, on the other hand, needs to slow down and do more research before taking action. Following is Siegelman's self-assessment exercise:[10]

Although people are rarely consistent in their decision-making styles, most of us can detect some regularity in the way we make important decisions. Think of the important life decisions you have made (e.g., marriage, divorce, major moves, career changes), and then answer the following questions. You may not answer some with complete confidence, but give the answers that come closest to what you believe. This is not a test; it is just a device to help you understand your own decision-making behavior. For each dimension, choose the one response out of three that best describes how you usually respond in making a big decision.

I. Attitude toward change
   1. I prefer security to novelty.
   2. I value security and novelty about equally.
   3. I prefer novelty to security.

II. Search strategy
   1. I make a quick overall survey of possibilities hoping that something will hit me.

2. I keep producing and then going over my possible choices.
3. I think of a number of alternatives but stop after reasonable search.

III. Attention to feelings
1. I decide among alternatives not only by reasoning but by taking my feelings into account.
2. I make major decisions almost exclusively on the basis of my feelings.
3. I mistrust my feelings as a basis for a major decision; I try to use reason almost entirely.

IV. Decision rule
1. I believe there is one right decision, and it is my job to dig it out.
2. I believe there is no one right decision; I just need to find one that is good enough.
3. I believe in choosing the first decision that really grabs me.

V. Sense of consequence
1. I don't try to predict the consequences of my decision because I expect things will work out OK.
2. I do think about consequences, tending to focus on the bad things that might happen.
3. I try to think of both the good and bad consequences of my decision.

VI. Predecision emotions
1. In thinking about taking a risky step, I feel mostly anxiety.
2. In thinking about taking a risky step, I feel a mixture of anxiety and excitement.
3. In thinking about taking a risky step, I feel mostly excitement.

VII. Time expended in decision-making process
   1. I usually make decisions — even big ones — quickly.
   2. I usually take a fairly long time to make big decisions.
   3. I usually take a very long time to make big decisions.

VIII. Attitude toward new information
   1. I will consider new information even after I've arrived at a probable decision.
   2. I'm not interested in getting new information after I've made a probable decision.
   3. I feel compelled either to seek out new information or to shut it out after I've made a probable decision.

IX. Postdecision strategy
   1. Once I've made a decision, I usually don't think about it before launching into action.
   2. Once I've made a decision, I often experience serious doubts and may change my mind.
   3. Once I've made a decision, I usually rally behind it after rechecking.

X. Evaluating the outcome of a risky decision
   1. After I have acted on the decision, I tend to worry or regret that I didn't do something else.
   2. After I have acted on the decision, I tend to put it out of my mind.
   3. After I have acted on the decision, I tend to think about what I have learned from it.

Scoring: Tally the number of A responses, B responses, and C responses using the following guide:

I. — 1. A   2. B   3. C
II. — 1. C   2. A   3. B
III. — 1. B   2. C   3. A

IV. — 1. A	2. B	3. C
V. — 1. C	2. A	3. B
VI. — 1. A	2. B	3. C
VII. — 1. C	2. B	3. A
VIII. — 1. B	2. C	3. A
IX. — 1. C	2. A	3. B
X. — 1. A	2. C	3. B

Style A: The anxious risk taker makes big decisions with great effort, is afraid of making mistakes, takes lots of time, and tends to ruminate and worry about the outcome.

Style B: The balanced risk taker makes big decisions fairly slowly, is more concerned with reasonably good outcomes than with fear of failure or the need to make a good decision, and tends to plan and to review but without worrying too much.

Style C: The careless risk taker makes big decisions quickly with little experience of mixed feelings, may feel "inappropriately optimistic," and spends little time in introspection or evaluation.

Most people evidence a mixture of styles. The average number of A responses is 6.7. The average number of B responses is 2.3. And the average number of C responses is 1.0. The goal is to be balanced.

Develop an assertion message. Michael Baer, a former pastor in Texas, suggests a technique he learned from Robert Bolton's *People Skills.*[11] Professional managers use a simple, brief formula to teach employees basic confrontational technique. It provides a framework for saying what needs to be said without sending the wrong messages. Essentially it is made up of three parts:

"When you (insert the other person's behavior), I feel (explain how it makes you feel) because (give a specific negative effect of their behavior)."

1. The formula gives a nonemotional description of the

behavior you want to see changed. For example, you might say, "When you come late to board meetings . . ." Keep it specific and do not exaggerate by saying things like "When you are always late for board meetings." Few people are always late.

2. State your *feelings* about the behavior. For example, you might say, "When you come late to the board meetings, I feel angry." This lets the other person know you care.

3. Finally, point out the results of the undesirable behavior. You might say, "When you come late to the board meetings, I feel angry because it causes all of us to get home late."

The formula is not a panacea but a beginning toward confronting others in situations with potential risk. By mastering the technique, some of your reluctance to confront may be dispelled.

The Personal Costs and Benefits

In our survey, pastors who said they made no tough decisions, in any of the categories, during a year were more likely to be fired than pastors who could identify such decisions. Pastors willing to face decisions last longer.

Yet longevity is not the only indicator of fallout from making or not making difficult decisions. There are other, less obvious factors. To identify those, the survey asked a series of questions about the toll risky decisions take on the leaders' personal well-being, their ministry effectiveness, and their families.

The good news from the survey results is that when a tough decision is over, most of the pastors who stay (85 percent) and even most of those who leave (81 percent) see benefits from the process they have been through.

Surprisingly, tough decisions cost pastors who stayed more *personal* pain than those who were forced to leave. Seventy-five percent of the pastors who stayed after a tough decision said the process took a toll on their physical/mental/emotional health compared to only 63 percent of the pastors who were fired. The fired pastors did perceive the cost to their children to be more expensive. But even here the reported difference was small. Ministry decision making takes a toll on everyone in the pastor's family, no matter what the outcome of the decision.

Ministerial effectiveness, as perceived by the pastor involved, always suffers. Both fired and nonfired pastors recognized that a church in pain cannot serve as well as a church in good health.

Conclusion

Several truths emerge: No one loves confrontation. For some it is worse than others. Confrontations must be made. There will be personal and ministry costs, as well as benefits.

Once these truths are accepted and weighed, it is perhaps helpful to go through one final checklist of questions to help determine *Just what can I handle personally?*

Will this risk make me satisfied if it is successful? How do I know? What else would satisfy me? Do I need to risk for that?

Do I allow myself to feel hurt, sad, angry, anxious, or joyous?

Am I aware of my moods and how they influence my actions? Do I recognize my feelings? Can I take a rejection in this case? If I am rejected, how will I act?

What are the limits to the amount of emotion I can show without adversely affecting the body of Christ?

Many of those responding to the survey spoke poignantly about the hurt, pain, and healing of a risk gone wrong, but none more so than a pastor's wife whose husband had lost a battle with an elder, which forced them to leave their church:

"I felt a sense of betrayal, a sense that grew on me. After we announced our resignation, we continued to serve from the end of August through December. I read negative feelings into a lot of what people did. If they didn't say anything, I thought they were thinking bad thoughts about us. I became suspicious and withdrawn. It could have gotten pretty bad, but the Lord provided insight for me in a dream.

"One night I fell asleep crying out to God and I dreamed of dried cornstalks in my garden. Ordinarily in the fall I cut those stalks into pieces. In my dream, the Lord gave me a choice: I could cut up the stalks and leave them on the ground, or I could till them into the soil, nourishing it for next year.

"I saw clearly that those cornstalks were like my anger. I could leave the pieces lying on the ground to pick up and throw at anyone who came near me. Or I could plow them under and use this experience to help me grow in the future. I learned that painful experiences could be something nourishing to me and others through me — if I let them. Or I could keep those pieces of pain and anger in my life and allow the resentment to remain. I remember making a deliberate choice that night: 'Lord, I want this painful time to nourish my life, but you're going to have to help me because I'm too angry to do it myself.'

"God has indeed helped that process. The pain was real, and I wouldn't want to go through it again. But God does help make everything work together for good."

THE RISK PROFILE

Take calculated risks. That is quite different from being rash.

GEORGE S. PATTON

Is there a way to tell how risky a decision is? Perhaps. At least we can point to the statistical probability that a particular ministry decision will ultimately cause a pastor to leave a church. Pastors indicated they make only a few truly difficult decisions in a year. Yet those are tough indeed. The average tenure of a pastor in a church is somewhere between four and five years. Often moves are made because of decisions that have led to disaster.

Although this is a scary prospect, it is not cause to run, but to take stock. Every pastor faces strong pressures and strong-willed parishioners. And every decision can involve hundreds of major and minor variables. Many of these *cannot* be quantified:

— how your particular church board operates
— the characteristics of every individual on your board
— the unique characteristics of the staff
— the number of powerful families in your church
— the characteristics of those families
— the history of the issue being decided.

Many can be quantified, however. We have compiled the results of our survey into a practical self-test. Ask yourself the following questions about yourself and your church environment. Circle your answers as you go through the test. Following the test, you'll find instructions on how to score your answers. (The survey from which we gathered the information used to contruct this test, along with more detailed analysis of the results, may be found in the Appendix.)

Questions

1. What is your education? (Circle all that apply to you.)

    1a. No higher education degree
    1b. Bible college degree
    1c. Liberal arts degree
    1d. Seminary degree
    1e. Non-seminary master's degree
    1f. Doctorate

2. What is your current church membership size?

    2a. less than 100
    2b. 100–199
    2c. 200–499
    2d. 500 or more

3. How long have you been at this church?

    3a. Less than one year
    3b. 1–2 years
    3c. 3–4 years
    3d. 5 or more years

4. What is your age?

    4a. 30 or under
    4b. 31–40

4c. 41–50
4d. 51–60
4e. over 60

5. Which church is this in your ministry history?

5a. My first church
5b. My second church
5c. My third church
5d. Fourth or later church

6. What do you believe to be your dominant gifts/talents in ministry?

6a. Preaching
6b. Teaching
6c. Administration
6d. Counseling
6e. Pastoral ministry (visitation, etc.)
6f. Evangelism
6g. Music
6h. Other

7. Do you use a biblical character (such as Jesus, Paul, or Moses) as a model for decision making?

7a. Yes
7b. No

8. How many times in a typical year are you required to make decisions that you know will upset, offend, or bring disagreement from people in the congregation?

a. THEOLOGICAL DECISIONS:
(e.g., to take a stand on eschatology, spiritual gifts, divorce/remarriage, etc., that differs from some members' views.)

8a1. None
8a2. 1–2 per year
8a3. 3–4 per year
8a4. 5 or more per year

b. INSTITUTIONAL/ORGANIZATIONAL DECISIONS:
(e.g., to recommend a ministry program that clashes with the polity or tradition of the church.)

8b1. None
8b2. 1–2 per year
8b3. 3–4 per year
8b4. 5 or more per year

c. INTERPERSONAL DECISIONS:
(e.g., handling a counseling session in a way that offends a church family, or having a conflict with a board member.)

8c1. None
8c2. 1–2 per year
8c3. 3–4 per year
8c4. 5 or more per year

Scoring Instructions

Now that you've completed the test, use these guidelines to score your answers:

RISK POINTS: If you are facing a risky decision at this time, each risk point increases your chance of ultimately having to leave your current ministry position as a result of it.

SAFETY POINTS: Each safety point decreases your chance of ultimately having to leave your current ministry position as a result of a difficult decision.

(Not all of the answers from the questions above were shown to have a measurable level of riskiness or safety. The ones that do are listed below.)

RISK POINTS	SAFETY POINTS	ANSWERS	
-2		1a.	No higher education degree
	+2	1c.	Liberal arts degree
	+2	1d.	Seminary degree
-2		1e.	Non-seminary master's degree
-4		1f.	Doctorate
	+2	2b.	100–199
-3		2c.	200–499
-2		3b.	1–2 years
	+2	3d.	5 or more years
	+3	5b.	My second church
-2		5c.	My third church
-2		5d.	My fourth or later church
	+3	6a.	Preaching
-3		6b.	Teaching (-3 *only* if preaching is not also listed)
	+3	7a.	Yes, I use a biblical character as a model for decision making.
-2		7b.	No, I don't use a biblical character as a model for decision making.
-2		8a1.	No theological decisions per year
	+3	8a2.	1–2 per year
-3		8c1.	No interpersonal decisions per year

| +2 | 8c3. 3–4 interpersonal decisions per year |
| +2 | 8c4. 5 or more interpersonal decisions per year |

How to Calculate Your Score

Add the safety points and subtract the risk points. The more positive your total score, the more safe is your current environment in ministry decision making. Use the following guidelines to evaluate your score.

SCORE	RISK EVALUATION
+14 and higher	A very high score. — You are in a relatively risk-free environment. — Continue to be sensitive to your flock as you also continue your vigorous approach to tough decision making.
+6 to +13	An average score. — Take stock of the currently risky factors about your background and/or your church environment. — Evaluate your own decision-making process to see how it could be strengthened.
+5 or less	A very risky score. — Look closely at the combination of your background and your current church environment to see where your dangers lie. — Be aware of the dangers. — As you evaluate your own decision-making process, seek out advice from

experienced pastors on decision making itself as well as the tough decisions you face.

FOURTEEN

KNOWLEDGE, ACTION, AND GOD

Working hard to make a decision work is even more important than making the decision in the first place. One of the dangers is people making a decision, then thinking, 'Oh, that's it,' when the thing has only just started.

LORD PENNOCK

Measuring the risk of difficult decisions does not guarantee our decisions will be good ones. Just as risk stalks our every action, so fallibility will always characterize the leadership we give our churches. We make mistakes.

Yet our mistakes need not consume us. We gain some comfort by knowing we are not alone in this human enterprise of making errors. Consider the record company that turned down the Beatles, the seventeen publishers who rejected the best-selling novel *M*A*S*H*, the editor of the *San Francisco Examiner* who told Rudyard Kipling his writing was "simply ridiculous." These monumental errors of judgment remind us that mistakes are inevitable. In a small way, that knowledge makes our misreading of a counseling situation, our failure to fully step up to the challenge of a difficult sermon topic, or our well-intentioned *faux pas* at a church social seem more manageable.

We cannot hide behind this knowledge of our fallibility, however. We may not be able to error-proof our ministries, but we can certainly improve our fielding averages. The thesis of this book has been that one good way to hone decision-making abilities is to measure the risk element in each decision. Knowing when to jump into a tough situation and when to bide one's time and gather more information and support can make the difference between a good decision and a foolhardy one.

If our survey information is any indication, most local church leaders already make far more good than foolhardy decisions. Respondents told of successfully dealing with problems ranging from choir robe controversies ("Do we really *need* new choir robes?") to telling 77-year-old organists afflicted with arthritis that their skills no longer aid worship ("It's like being asked to execute your grandmother") to negotiating a truce between one group of families who had discovered the more dramatic gifts of the Spirit and the thirty other families in the church who weren't interested in any gifts except those that came from Santa Claus.

Yet, when we asked, "Please describe your biggest mistake in ministry," every one of the returned surveys told of a decision gone sour, an oversight that in retrospect seemed obvious, a minor ripple that turned into a cascade of trouble. And frequently the descriptions ended with a comment like, "I sure don't want to go through that again." One major impression bled through: help of any sort would be readily accepted.

Our personal interviews accentuated that impression. When to take a risk haunts many local church leaders. They alternate between what often turns out to be brash boldness and terminal tactfulness. With no clear strategy on when to act and when not to, frustration threatens every situation. Too frequently it dominates.

One pastor told of successfully confronting a couple who had thwarted effective ministry in his tiny church for years. But instead of satisfaction at its conclusion, he felt only fear and anxiety that it would happen again, that the next difficult decision he would have to face, he wouldn't be able to step up to:

"The trouble was I didn't choose the confrontation. I didn't prepare for it. Throughout the whole situation I never felt in control. I felt like I was being swept away by events and people. I didn't like that. I have always had a sign on my office wall that reads, FIGHT SIN, NOT PEOPLE. I suppose that can be good advice, but ministry means a little of both, and sometimes I can't tell the two apart."

Our hope is that the insights we have outlined in this book will give that sense of control. The preceding chapters have provided a program of action that can help measure risk and provide the information one needs to confront head-on both sin and people.

The program cannot do it all. Life's most difficult issues don't lend themselves to one-two-three solutions. Such steps put us in position to solve problems, but other elements enter in. One of those other elements is hard work. Successful decision making is made up of preparation, courage, and hard work, but the greatest of these is hard work.

One of my favorite Bible settings is Moses standing on the wrong side of the Red Sea, the side that has an angry, well-trained army of Egyptians bearing down on his ill-equipped band of freedom seekers. "General" Moses is not quite sure what to do. Perhaps he was thinking, *What would Joseph have done in this situation?* He probably couldn't recall anything, however, with his followers screaming sarcastically in his ear, "Was it because there were no graves in Egypt that you brought us to the desert to die?"

Finally, Moses remembered enough about God's sustaining power to blurt out, "Stand firm. . . . The Lord will fight for you; you need only to be still."[1]

Standing still and letting the Lord do all the work was not the program God had in mind, however. I love the Lord's answer: "Why are you crying out to me? Tell the Israelites to move on." Having stimulated them to action and spurred them to move beyond their paralyzing fear, he then parted the sea, and the Israelites escaped.

After deciding to take a risk, we can't sit back and think the job is done. We are still required to make our decisions work.

Having said that, we must not ignore the power we have available to us in the Holy Spirit. Good ministry and good prayer lives go together. Few of us would survive in ministry if it wasn't for this inexhaustible source of power. It's been said that without devotion, knowledge and action are cold and dry and may even become shackles. The knowledge of when to take a ministerial risk is essential; the willingness to invest the hard work to make that risk work is crucial. But only God's blessing insures any kind of effective ministry.

We pray for that blessing for your ministry.

APPENDIX

The empirical foundations of the risk theory and risk scale developed in this book rest upon the statistical results of a survey questionnaire devised by Virginia Vagt and Terry Muck in the summer of 1985 and sent to a random sample of pastors and local church leaders. A history of that research:

A test questionnaire was sent to two groups of approximately twenty-five local church leaders each. One group was made up of pastors who had not been fired or pressured to leave a church at any time during their ministry. The other group was made up of pastors known to have been fired or pressured to leave a church at some time during their ministry.

The questionnaire was pretested with these two groups with two objectives. One, to find out if the groups' answers would indicate a statistically significant differentiation. They did.

Second, the pretest tested the wording and understandability of the questions. As a result, significant rewriting and readjusting of the questions were done to make the survey as clear as possible.

The revised questionnaire was mailed to 946 *LEADERSHIP* Journal pastor subscribers in August, 1985. And 171 questionnaires (18 percent) were returned. (In previous research of *LEADERSHIP* and CHRISTIANITY TODAY subscribers, we have found pastors to be poorer respondents than lay people. To help our response rate, we sent an advance postcard to our sample and included an incentive, a ballpoint pen, in the survey mailing.)

The full questionnaire follows:

LEADERSHIP SURVEY

To prime your thinking, please read through the following types of ministry decisions.

A. THEOLOGICAL
These decisions stem *primarily* from theological concerns. For example:
- you had to take a stand on a crucial issue such as eschatology, spiritual gifts, divorce/remarriage, etc., that was different from some people in the congregation/denomination.

B. INSTITUTIONAL/ORGANIZATIONAL
These decisions stem *primarily* from a concern for the effectiveness of the congregation. For example:
- you had to recommend a ministry program that clashed with the polity or tradition of the church
- you sought to curb dissension that was threatening the body
- you had to let an organist go because poor performance was negatively affecting worship
- you had a conflict with the board about a policy matter, etc.

C. INTERPERSONAL
These decisions stem *primarily* from a conflict that involves personal misunderstanding/animosity either between you and another party in the church, or two independent parties.
For example:
- you experienced conflict with a staff member or volunteer leader
- someone in a counseling situation felt offended by your style of ministry
- you experienced personal conflict with a board member
- you were called upon to arbitrate a real estate disagreement between two church members.

Please answer the following questions about decisions you've made. Use extra sheets if necessary to answer as fully as possible.

1. Describe the toughest decision you have ever made in ministry that *didn't* result in your leaving a church.

    Before you describe it, using the definitions above, how would you categorize this decision?
    ☐₁ Theological   ☐₃ Interpersonal
    ☐₂ Institutional/organizational   ☐₄ Other, please describe:

2. What, if any, were the costs of that decision or decision-making process? (Please check and describe all that applied to your situation.)

PERSONAL COST
☐₁ No real personal cost
☐₂ Toll on my physical/mental/emotional health, please describe:

☐₃ Toll on my spouse/our marriage, please describe:

☐₄ Toll on my children, please describe:

☐₅ Toll on my spiritual life, please describe:

☐₆ Toll on my ministry effectiveness, please describe:

☐₇ Other, please describe:

COST TO INDIVIDUALS IN THE CHURCH
☐₁ No real cost to individuals
☐₂ The individuals involved left the church
☐₃ Toll on these individuals' physical/mental/emotional health
☐₄ Other, please describe:

COST TO THE EFFECTIVENESS OF THE CHURCH
☐₁ No real cost to the church
☐₂ Lapse of effectiveness of one or more ministries in the church, please describe:

☐₃ Other people in the congregation left the church because of this situation, please describe:

☐₄ Other, please describe:

OTHER
☐₁ Other cost, please describe:

3. What, if any, were the benefits of this decision or decision-making process you described in question one?

PERSONAL BENEFITS:

BENEFITS TO INDIVIDUALS IN THE CHURCH:

BENEFITS TO THE CHURCH'S EFFECTIVENESS:

4. Because you as pastor or pastoral staff had to take a position you knew to be incompatible with the wishes of the church, have you ever left a church or been forced to resign?

☐₁ Yes   ☐₂ No (If no, please skip to question 9.)

If yes, how many times during your ministry has the above occurred?

☐ 1   ☐ 2   ☐ 3   ☐ 4 or more

Check the major type of position/decision that you took preceding each departure.

	First Departure	Second Departure	Third Departure	Fourth Departure
a. Theological				
b. Institutional/ organizational				
c. Interpersonal				
d. Other, please describe:				

5. Describe *one* of these departures in detail, using extra sheets if necessary.

Were there other factors that could have contributed to your leaving?

6. Looking back, what, if anything, would you have done differently?

Do you think this action on your part would have prolonged your ministry at that church? How long?

7. In addition to loss of that pastorate, what other losses/costs were experienced, if any? (Please check and describe all that applied to your situation.)

PERSONAL COST

$\square_1$ Toll on my physical/mental/emotional health, please describe:

$\square_2$ Toll on my spouse/our marriage, please describe:

$\square_3$ Toll on my children, please describe:

$\square_4$ Toll on my spiritual life, please describe:

$\square_5$ Toll on my ministry effectiveness in subsequent ministries, please describe:

$\square_6$ Other, please describe:

COST TO INDIVIDUALS IN THE CHURCH

$\square_1$ No real cost to individuals
$\square_2$ The individuals involved left the church
$\square_3$ Toll on these individuals' physical/mental/emotional health
$\square_4$ Other, please describe:

COST TO THE EFFECTIVENESS OF THE CHURCH

$\square_1$ No real cost to the church
$\square_2$ Lapse of effectiveness of one or more ministries in the church, please describe:

$\square_3$ Other people in the congregation left the church because of this situation, please describe:

$\square_4$ Other, please describe:

OTHER

$\square_1$ Other cost, please describe:

8. What, if any, were the **benefits** of the decision or decision-making process that led to your leaving?

PERSONAL BENEFITS:

BENEFITS TO INDIVIDUALS IN THE CHURCH:

BENEFITS TO THE CHURCH'S EFFECTIVENESS:

9. How many times in a typical year are you required to make decisions that you know will upset, offend, or bring disagreement from people in the congregation?

CHECK **ONE** FOR EACH OF THE FOLLOWING TYPES OF DECISIONS.

THEOLOGICAL DECISIONS
(e.g., I took a theological stance on a crucial issue such as eschatology, gifts, divorce/remarriage, etc., that was different from some people in the congregation.)
☐ None   ☐ 1 per year   ☐ 2 per year   ☐ 3 per year
☐ 4 per year   ☐ 5 or more per year

INSTITUTIONAL/ORGANIZATIONAL DECISIONS
(e.g., I recommended a ministry program that clashed with the polity or tradition of the church; I sought to curb some dissension; I had to let the organist go because poor performance was negatively affecting worship.)
☐ None   ☐ 1 per year   ☐ 2 per year   ☐ 3 per year
☐ 4 per year   ☐ 5 or more per year

INTERPERSONAL DECISIONS
(e.g., I handled a counseling session in a way that offended a church family; I had a personal conflict with a board member.)
☐ None   ☐ 1 per year   ☐ 2 per year
☐ 3 per year   ☐ 4 per year   ☐ 5 or more per year

10. What do you believe to be your dominant gifts/talents in ministry?
☐$_1$ Administration
☐$_2$ Preaching
☐$_3$ Counseling (structured counseling ministry)
☐$_4$ Pastoral ministry (visitation, etc.)
☐$_5$ Evangelism
☐$_6$ Teaching
☐$_7$ Music
☐$_8$ Other, please specify:

Which ministry area is your *strongest* ministry gift/talent?

Which of the above ministry areas are you *least* gifted in?

11. What is your church polity:
☐₁ Congregational   ☐₂ Episcopal   ☐₃ Presbyterian

12. Who have been your biblical models in decision making? Why?

13. What other resources does a local church leader have in decision making?

14. What is your ministry history? (Describe your first church after #1 and so on through to your present church. If you had a non-parish ministry or another occupation before, during, or after any of these churches, please briefly describe in sequence.)

Denomination of Church	State	SUBURBAN* URBAN RURAL	Size of Member- ship	Date Started	Date Left	Reason For Leaving
1.		S U R*				
2.		S U R				
3.		S U R				
4.		S U R				
5.		S U R				
6.		S U R				
7.		S U R				

* Please circle S, U, or R for each church location.

15. What is your religious affiliation?
    - $\Box_1$ Southern Baptist
    - $\Box_2$ Other Baptist
    - $\Box_3$ Church of Christ/Christian
    - $\Box_4$ Christian & Missionary Alliance
    - $\Box_5$ Evangelical Free
    - $\Box_6$ Lutheran
    - $\Box_7$ Mennonite/Brethren/Anabaptist
    - $\Box_8$ United Methodist
    - $\Box_9$ Wesleyan/Holiness/Other Methodist
    - $\Box_{10}$ Nazarene
    - $\Box_{11}$ Pentecostal/Charismatic
    - $\Box_{12}$ Presbyterian/Reformed
    - $\Box_{13}$ Independent/nondenominational
    - $\Box_{14}$ Other (please specify):

16. What is your age? $\Box$ 30 or under $\Box$ 31–40 $\Box$ 41–50
    $\Box$ 51–60 $\Box$ 61–70 $\Box$ Over 70

17. What is your sex? $\Box_1$ male $\Box_2$ female

18. What is your marital status?
    $\Box_1$ Single $\Box_2$ Married $\Box_3$ Divorced
    $\Box_4$ Separated $\Box_5$ Widowed

19. What is your education? (Check all that apply to you.)
    $\Box_1$ Bible institute or college degree $\Box_4$ Other master's degree
    $\Box_2$ Liberal arts college degree $\Box_5$ Doctorate
    $\Box_3$ Seminary degree

20. If you would be willing to be called by one of our editors for more information, please add your name and phone number below. Thank you.

    Name: Phone: (   )

Summary of Survey Findings

The following numbers are all percentages and are the result of cross-tabulations run between two groups of respondents (each survey response became a member of one of two groups):

Fired: those respondents who have had to leave a church as a result of a tough decision;

Not fired: those respondents who have not had to leave a church as a result of a tough decision.

After the cross-tabulations of each question, there are some observations. Not all of these observations were strong enough statistically to become part of the Risk Profile (self-test) that appeared in chapter 13. In the Risk Profile we used only our strongest statistics, and after constructing the Profile we revalidated the test and the scoring scale by applying the Risk Profile to the surveys of fired and not-fired groups.

DEMOGRAPHICS

Demographic variables of a church or the pastor seemed to have some impact on whether or not a pastor will have to leave a church after a risky decision is made. All numbers are percentages.

MARITAL STATUS

Only 3 percent of our returns were from single people. Therefore, we had insufficient data to compare being married to being single as far as their impact on risk taking. (No fired pastors were single.)

EDUCATION

Fired	Not Fired	Education
9	0	No degree
25	34	Bible college degree
33	45	Liberal arts degree
58	67	Seminary degree
31	16	Master's degree
25	9	Doctorate

Pastors who have a Bible college, liberal arts, or seminary degree have less of a chance of having to leave a church than those who don't. Pastors who have a master's or doctoral degree have a greater chance of leaving a church as a result of a risky decision.

GEOGRAPHIC LOCATION OF CHURCH

Fired	Not Fired	Location
6	22	Mid Atlantic
21	15	Southern
36	43	Midwestern
0	1	Rocky Mountain
6	8	Southwestern
27	11	Pacific Coast

We had insufficient data to know if geographic location has an impact on pastoral risk taking.

COMMUNITY TYPE

Fired	Not Fired	Community Type
46	46	Suburban
29	21	Urban
26	33	Rural

Community type does not seem to be a factor in the likelihood of a pastor having to leave a church as a result of a risky decision.

CHURCH SIZE

Fired	Not Fired	Size of Church Membership
36	32	less than 100
22	35	100-199
33	19	200-499
8	14	500 or more

Compared to pastors of churches of 0–199 members, pastors of churches with 200–499 members have a greater chance of having to leave. We had insufficient data from churches of 500 or more members to know if that church size has an impact on whether a pastor will have to leave as a result of a decision.

MINISTRY TENURE

Fired	Not Fired	Ministry Length
3	5	Less than 1 year
47	39	1–2 years
22	21	3–4 years
28	36	5 or more years

In this sample, pastors tended to leave a church more often between the first and second years. Pastors would be wise to realize that for many reasons they are likely to leave between the first and second years. Making a risky decision might be one of several factors that will contribute to leaving.

PASTOR'S AGE

Fired	Not Fired	Pastor's Age
33	34	30 or under
33	40	31–40
28	15	41–50
6	10	51–60

We had insufficient data to include the 61–70 age group in this table. It appears that pastors have a greater chance of having to leave a church when they are between 41 and 50 than at any other age and that young pastors are another high risk group. We are tentative about this statistic because our post-test revalidation of this finding was inconclusive. More research needs to be done on this factor.

CAREER ORDER

Fired	Not Fired	Career Order
41	41	First church

19	34	Second church
22	15	Third church
19	10	Fourth or later church

There is less chance that a pastor will have to leave his or her second church due to a risky decision made than there is having to leave his or her first or third church.

SEX
We had insufficient data to determine whether gender has an impact on a pastor's chances of having to leave a church as a result of a risky decision.

DENOMINATION
For seventeen of the denominations represented, we had insufficient data to determine whether denominational affiliation has an impact on a pastor's chances of having to leave a church as a result of a risky decision.

PASTORAL GIFTS
Following are answers to the question, "What do you believe to be your dominant gifts/talents in ministry?"

Fired	Not Fired	Gifts
26	38	Preaching
46	25	Teaching
9	16	Administration
9	3	Counseling
9	9	Pastoral

Pastors who perceive their dominant ministry gift is teaching have a greater chance of having to leave a church due to a risky decision than pastors who perceive preaching is their dominant ministry gift. The number of responses to the other gifts makes analysis of their relative importance problematic. Music and evangelism received fewer responses as dominant gifts/talents. These did not have any bearing on whether a pastor had to leave a church.

CHURCH POLITY

Fired	Not Fired	Polity
64	68	Congregational
14	14	Episcopal
22	18	Presbyterian

Church polity does not seem to be a factor in a pastor's chances of having to leave a church as a result of a risky decision.

BIBLICAL MODELS
Answers to the question, "Who have been your biblical models in decision making?"

Fired	Not Fired	Model
12	39	Jesus
39	49	Paul
9	17	Moses
15	12	Prophets

Pastors who use Jesus as a biblical model in decision making have less of a chance of having to leave a church than pastors who use other biblical models.

TYPE OF DECISIONS
Following is a comparison of the answers Not-Fired pastors gave to Question #1, "Describe the toughest decision you have ever made," with answers Fired pastors gave to Question #4, "Check the major type of position/decision that you took preceding each departure."

Fired	Not Fired	Decision
29	29	Theological
29	33	Institutional/organizational
35	35	Interpersonal
6	3	Other

The type of decision does not seem to have an impact on a pastor's chances of having to leave a church as a result of taking a risky position. Frequency (and thus, implicitly, proper identification of problems) seems to be the determinative factor.

FREQUENCY OF DECISIONS
Following are answers to the question, "How many times in a typical year are you required to make decisions that you know will upset, offend, or bring disagreement from people in the congregation?"

Theological Decisions

Fired	Not Fired	Times during the year
24	14	No times during the year
29	41	1 decision per year
12	21	2 decisions per year
21	7	3 decisions per year
15	17	4 or more decisions per year

Institutional/Organizational Decisions

Fired	Not Fired	Times during the year
20	16	No times during the year
40	38	1 decision per year
17	19	2 decisions per year
11	16	3 decisions per year
11	13	4 or more decisions per year

Interpersonal Decisions

Fired	Not Fired	Times during the year
21	16	No times during the year
32	26	1 decision per year
29	19	2 decisions per year
12	23	3 decisions per year
6	16	4 or more decisions per year
15	17	5 or more decisions per year

COSTS — PERSONAL

Following are answers to Question #2, "In addition to the loss of that pastorate, what other losses/costs were experienced, if any?" (Asked of pastors who had been fired.)

Also included are answers to Question #7, "What, if any, were the costs of that decision or decision-making process?" (Asked of pastors about the toughest decision they had made that didn't lead to firing.)

Fired	Not Fired	Personal Cost
63	75	Toll on my physical/mental/emotional health
31	52	Toll on my ministry effectiveness
44	47	Toll on my spouse/our marriage
28	34	Toll on my spiritual life
19	15	Toll on my children

The decision-making process is expensive whether a pastor ends up leaving or staying. But surprisingly, the process for the pastor who stays is reportedly tougher than for the pastor who ultimately leaves. Only the pastor's perception of the costs to his or her children were reported higher for pastors who had to leave. But even here the difference is very small. Ministry decision making takes its toll on everyone in the pastor's family, no matter what the outcome of the decision.

COSTS — CORPORATE

Fired	Not Fired	Cost to Individuals in the Church
28	16	No real cost to individuals in the church
44	53	The individuals involved left the church
19	28	Toll on these individuals' physical/ mental/emotional health

COSTS — MINISTRY EFFECTIVENESS

Fired	Not Fired	Cost to the ministry effectiveness of the church
44	37	No real cost to the church
34	43	Lapse of effectiveness of ministry

Pastors who stay report higher costs to others involved in the decision-making process than those who leave, perhaps due to several factors. On the one hand, it may be that leaving or being forced to leave is the easy way out. At the church where the pastor has to leave, other individuals in the church and the church's effectiveness are not as taxed as in the church where the pastor and the church work through their tough times. On the other hand, it could be that pastors who leave, or are forced to leave, are less sensitive to the pain that others and the church experience in a decision-making process.

BENEFITS

Fired	Not Fired	Benefits
81	85	Personal benefits
63	66	Benefits to individuals in church
56	73	Benefits to church's effectiveness

Most pastors, whether they had to leave or not, reported personal benefits to themselves and to individuals in the church as a result of a tough decision-making process. And in the pastors' eyes, as would be expected, the payoffs of decision making are higher at the church where the pastor stays than in the church where the pastor has to leave.

NOTES

CHAPTER 1

Helen Keller, *The Story of My Life* (New York: Doubleday and Company, Inc., 1954).

1. We have changed the names and identifying details in this story.

CHAPTER 2

J. L. Cranmer-Byng, ed., *Burmese Proverbs* (London: John Murray, 1962), 23.

1. Robert Jackall, "Moral Mazes: Bureaucracy and Managerial Work," *Harvard Business Review* (September/October 1983): 126.
2. Donald McCoy, *Calvin Coolidge: The Quiet President* (New York: Macmillan Company, 1967), 86–95.
3. August Heckscher, "The Risk-Takers," *Christian Science Monitor* (19 June 1981): 20.
4. John Urquhart and Klaus Heilmann, *Risk Watch: The Art of Life* (New York: Facts on File Publications, 1984), 21ff.
5. See Donald Attwater, *St. John Chrysostom* (Milwaukee: The Bruce Publishing Company, 1939).
6. See G. R. Potter, *Zwingli* (London: Cambridge University Press, 1976).

CHAPTER 3

George Herbert, "Jacula Prudentum," *Works* (London: Oxford University Press, 1941).

1. Robert J. Trotter, "Blackjack Behavior: When Rational Minds Go Bust," *Psychology Today* (October 1985): 14. See also Gideon Keren and Willem Wagenaar, "On the Psychology of Playing Blackjack," *Journal of Experimental Psychology* (June 1985): 133–157.
2. Names and some identifying details have been changed in this story.
3. Elsie Johnson, "Anticipatory Leadership," *Catalyst for Change* (Spring 1981): 27.

CHAPTER 4

Thomas Fuller, *The Virtuous Lady*. Quoted in Sydney Roberts, *Thomas Fuller: A Seventeenth Century Worthy* (Manchester: Manchester University Press, 1953).

1. Fred Craddock audio cassette, "Preaching as Storytelling" Workshop, *Preaching Today 23* (June, 1985).

CHAPTER 5

Quoted in James Hastings, *Great Prayer* (New York: Scribner and Sons, Inc., 1915), 16.

1. Jean-Pierre de Caussade, *The Sacrament of the Present Moment* (San Francisco: Harper & Row, 1982), 57.
2. Stanley Milgram, "The Perils of Obedience," *Harper's* (December 1973): 62–77. See also, Sarah McCarthy, "Why Johnny Can't Disobey," *The Humanist* (September/October 1979): 30–34.
3. David C. Bock and Neil Clark Warren, "Religious Belief as a Factor in Obedience to Destructive Commands," *Review of Religious Research* (Spring 1972): 185–190.

CHAPTER 6

Cardinal de Retz, *Memoires* (New York: French and European Publishers, n.d.).

1. George Marshall and David Poling, *Schweitzer: A Biography* (New York: Albert Schweitzer Fellowship, 1975), 252.
2. Charles Coleman, William Toomey, and Richard Woodland, "Cognition, Belief, and Behavior: A Study of Commitment to a Religious Institution," *Religious Education* (November/December 1975): 677.
3. Doyle Johnson, "Religious Commitment, Social Distance, and Authoritarianism," *Review of Religious Research* (Winter 1977): 99–112.
4. Dean M. Kelly, *Why Conservative Churches Are Growing* (New York: Harper & Row, 1977).
5. See Bruce Shelley, *Church History in Plain Language* (Waco, Texas: Word, 1982), 90–92.

CHAPTER 7

Alice Carey (source unknown)

1. Matthew 5:9.
2. John Chrysostom, "Homilies on Colossians (II)," *Nicene and Post Nicene Fathers XIII* (Grand Rapids, Michigan: Eerdmans Publishing Company, 1979), 268.
3. Franklin O. Nelson, former missionary to Burma. Interview with author, Minneapolis, Minnesota, August, 1984.
4. David Seamands, *Healing for Damaged Emotions* (Wheaton, Illinois: Victor Books, 1981).
5. Doris Donnelly, "The Human Side of Forgiveness and What It Tells Us about How God Forgives," *New Catholic World* (January/February 1984): 29.
6. J. I. Packer, *Knowing God* (Downers Grove, Illinois: InterVarsity Press, 1973), 245.
7. Jamie Buckingham, *Coping With Criticism* (South Plainfield, New Jersey: Bridge Publishing Company, 1978).

CHAPTER 8

William Penn, *Reflections and Maxims* (Philadelphia: Friends Book Store, 1886), 55.

1. Cited by Landon Y. Jones, "The Mid-Career Switch," *Esquire* (June 1982): 81.
2. Daniel Levinson, *The Seasons of a Man's Life* (New York: Ballantine, 1979).
3. Jonathan Edwards, *Religious Affections* (Portland, Oregon: Multnomah Press, 1984), 132–137.
4. Marguerite Wolf, "The Meaning of Security," *Parents Magazine* (December 1963): 64.

CHAPTER 9

William James, *The Will to Believe* (Cambridge, Massachusetts: Harvard University Press, 1979).

CHAPTER 10

Edward de Bono, *Tactics: The Art and Science of Success* (Boston: Little, Brown and Company, 1984), 115.

1. William Lowrance, *Of Acceptable Risk* (Los Altos, California: William Kaufmann, Inc., 1976), 155–173.
2. Many studies have been done of the so-called risky shift phenomenon. Some representatives: Dean G. Pruitt, "Choice Shifts in Group Discussion," *Journal of Personality and Social Psychology* (December 1971): 339–360; Richard Lilienthal, "Group Polarization (Risk Shift) in Led and Leaderless Group Discussions," *Psychological Reports 45* (1979): 168; James W. Dyson, Paul Godwin, Leo Hazlewood, "Group Composition, Leadership Orientation, and Decisional Outcomes," *Small Group Behavior* (February 1976): 114–127; Earl Cecil, Larry Cummings, Jerome Chertkoff, "Group Composition and Choice Shift: Implications for Administration," *Academy of Management Journal* (September 1973): 412–422. In this last article, the authors state five reasons why group decisions may shift toward either more risky or more conservative positions: 1) Making a

decision in a group allows for diffusion of responsibility in the event of a wrong decision; 2) Risky people are more influential than conservative people in group discussions; 3) Group discussion leads to deeper consideration of the possible pros and cons of a decision, leading to a higher level of risk; 4) Risk taking is socially desirable in our culture and socially desirable qualities are more likely to be expressed in a group than alone; 5) Generally, people will choose a risk level they believe is equal to or slightly greater than the risk the average person will take. Thus, when a group decision is made, members discovering they are more conservative than the average will become riskier.

CHAPTER 11

Thomas Paine, *Writings of Thomas Paine* (New York: AMS Press, Inc., 1896).

1. Quoted in Martin Marty's *Context*, (15 June 1985): 6.

CHAPTER 12

T. S. Eliot, in introduction to Baudelaire's *Intimate Journal* (San Francisco: City Lights Books, 1983).

1. I. D. Thomas, *A Word from the Wise* (Chicago: Moody Press, 1978), 140.
2. Proverbs 12:24, 27; 15:19; 18:9; 19:24; 21:25; 22:13; 24:30; 26:13, 14, 15; Matthew 25.
3. Epiphanius Wilson, ed., *Turkish Literature* (New York: Colonial Press, 1901), 12.
4. Frank Farley, "The Big T in Personality," *Psychology Today* (May 1986): 45–52.
5. W. Stuart Sewell, *Brief Biographies of Famous Men and Women* (New York: Garden City Publishing Company, 1949), 93.
6. Farley, "The Big T," 50.
7. John W. Atkinson, "Motivational Determinants of Risk-Taking Behavior," *Psychological Review* 64 (1957): 371.
8. Nathan Kogan and Michael Wallach, *Risk Taking* (New York: Holt, Rinehart and Winston, 1974).
9. David D. Burns, *Feeling Good: The New Mood Therapy* (New York: Signet Books, 1985).
10. Ellen Siegelman, *Personal Risk: Mastering Change in Love and Work* (New York: Harper & Row, 1983).
11. Robert Bolton, *People Skills* (New York: Prentice Hall, 1979).

CHAPTER 14

Quoted in Edward de Bono, *Tactics*, 132.

1. Exodus 14:10ff.

BIBLIOGRAPHY

Following is a select list of books that introduce the study of risk from biblical, psychological, and/or sociological points of view.

Arnold, John D., and Bert Tompkins. *How to Make the Right Decisions*. New York: Ballantine Books, 1982, 178 pages.

The authors outline a seven-step process for personal decision making. Written from a Christian perspective in a popular style.

Byrd, Richard. *A Guide to Personal Risk Taking*. Saranac Lake, New York: American Management Association, Inc., 1974, 357 pages.

A business-oriented book dealing with decisions about job and career.

Kogan, Nathan, and Michael Wallach. *Risk Taking: A Study of Cognition and Personality*. New York: Holt, Rinehart and Winston, 1964, 277 pages.

A detailed study of the psychology of the risk-taking personality. Authors are both academic researchers.

Lowrance, William W. *Of Acceptable Risk: Science and the Determination of Safety.* Los Altos, California: William Kaufmann, Inc., 1976, 180 pages.

A study of the science of risk taking, a growing profession that attempts to measure (and thus manage) risk for business and governmental policy makers. By a recognized expert in the field.

Siegelman, Ellen. *Personal Risk: Mastering Change in Love and Work.* New York: Harper & Row, 1983, 157 pages.

Written in the best tradition of popular self-help books.

Smedes, Lewis. *Choices: Making Right Decisions in a Complex World.* San Francisco: Harper & Row, 1986, 121 pages.

A Christian ethicist looks at the difficulties of personal decision making.

Urquhart, John, and Klaus Heilmann. *Risk Watch: The Odds of Life.* New York: Facts on File Publications, 1984, 214 pages.

Two sociologists examine the concept of risk in everyday living. They use statistics and research to put the "dangers" of everyday living in perspective.

DATE DUE			
OCT 28 '87			

DEMCO 38-297